The Grand Jury

CRIME, JUSTICE, AND PUNISHMENT

The Grand Jury

Leslie Berger

Austin Sarat, GENERAL EDITOR

CHELSEA HOUSE PUBLISHERS
Philadelphia

Chelsea House Publishers

Editor in Chief Stephen Reginald
Production Manager Pamela Loos
Art Director Sara Davis
Director of Photography Judy L. Hasday
Managing Editor James D. Gallagher
Senior Production Editor LeeAnne Gelletly

Staff for THE GRAND JURY

Series Editor John Ziff
Associate Art Director/Designer Takeshi Takahashi
Picture Researcher Gillian Speeth
Cover Illustrator Keith Trego

First Printing

1 3 5 7 9 8 6 4 2

The Chelsea House World Wide Web address is
http://www.chelseahouse.com

Library of Congress Cataloging-in-Publication Data

Berger, Leslie
The grand jury / Leslie Berger
    p. cm. — (Crime, justice, and punishment)
Includes bibliographical references and index.
Summary: Explains how the American grand jury system
operates and some of the abuses of this system, using classic
cases as illustrations.

ISBN 0-7910-4290-1 (hc)

1. Grand Jury—United States—Juvenile literature. 2.
Indictments—United States—Juvenile literature. [1.
Grand jury. 2. Indictments.] I. Title. II. Series.
KF9642.Z9 B47 1999
345.73'072—dc21   99-040243

21.95

Contents

Fears and Fascinations:
An Introduction to Crime,
Justice, and Punishment
Austin Sarat   7

CRIME, JUSTICE, AND PUNISHMENT

Fears and Fascinations:

An Introduction to Crime, Justice, and Punishment

By Austin Sarat

We live with crime and images of crime all around us. Crime evokes in most of us a deep aversion, a feeling of profound vulnerability, but it also evokes an equally deep fascination. Today, in major American cities the fear of crime is a major fact of life, some would say a disproportionate response to the realities of crime. Yet the fear of crime is real, palpable in the quickened steps and furtive glances of people walking down darkened streets. At the same time, we eagerly follow crime stories on television and in movies. We watch with a "who done it" curiosity, eager to see the illicit deed done, the investigation undertaken, the miscreant brought to justice and given his just deserts. On the streets the presence of crime is a reminder of our own vulnerability and the precariousness of our taken-for-granted rights and freedoms. On television and in the movies the crime story gives us a chance to probe our own darker motives, to ask "Is there a criminal within?" as well as to feel the collective satisfaction of seeing justice done.

Fear and fascination, these two poles of our engagement with crime, are, of course, only part of the story. Crime is, after all, a major social and legal problem, not just an issue of our individual psychology. Politicians today use our fear of, and fascination with, crime for political advantage. How we respond to crime, as well as to the political uses of the crime issue, tells us a lot about who we are as a people as well as what we value and what we tolerate. Is our response compassionate or severe? Do we seek to understand or to punish, to enact an angry vengeance or to rehabilitate and welcome the criminal back into our midst? The CRIME, JUSTICE, AND PUNISHMENT series is designed to explore these themes, to ask why we are fearful and fascinated, to probe the meanings and motivations of crimes and criminals and of our responses to them, and, finally, to ask what we can learn about ourselves and the society in which we live by examining our responses to crime.

Crime is always a challenge to the prevailing normative order and a test of the values and commitments of law-abiding people. It is sometimes a Raskolnikov-like act of defiance, an assertion of the unwillingness of some to live according to the rules of conduct laid out by organized society. In this sense, crime marks the limits of the law and reminds us of law's all-too-regular failures. Yet sometimes there is more desperation than defiance in criminal acts; sometimes they signal a deep pathology or need in the criminal. To confront crime is thus also to come face-to-face with the reality of social difference, of class privilege and extreme deprivation, of race and racism, of children neglected, abandoned, or abused whose response is to enact on others what they have experienced themselves. And occasionally crime, or what is labeled a criminal act, represents a call for justice, an appeal to a higher moral order against the inadequacies of existing law.

Figuring out the meaning of crime and the motivations of criminals and whether crime arises from defiance, desperation, or the appeal for justice is never an easy task. The motivations and meanings of crime are as varied as are the persons who engage in criminal conduct. They are as mysterious as any of the mysteries of the human soul. Yet the desire to know the secrets of crime and the criminal is a strong one, for in that knowledge may lie one step on the road to protection, if not an assurance of one's own personal safety. Nonetheless, as strong as that desire may be, there is no available technology that can allow us to know the whys of crime with much confidence, let alone a scientific certainty. We can, however, capture something about crime by studying the defiance, desperation, and quest for justice that may be associated with it. Books in the CRIME, JUSTICE, AND PUNISHMENT series will take up that challenge. They tell stories of crime and criminals, some famous, most not, some glamorous and exciting, most mundane and commonplace.

This series will, in addition, take a sober look at American criminal justice, at the procedures through which we investigate crimes and identify criminals, at the institutions in which innocence or guilt is determined. In these procedures and institutions we confront the thrill of the chase as well as the challenge of protecting the rights of those who defy our laws. It is through the efficiency and dedication of law enforcement that we might capture the criminal; it is in the rare instances of their corruption or brutality that we feel perhaps our deepest betrayal. Police, prosecutors, defense lawyers, judges, and jurors administer criminal justice and in their daily actions give substance to the guarantees of the Bill of Rights. What is an adversarial system of justice? How does it work? Why do we have it? Books in the CRIME, JUSTICE, AND PUNISHMENT series will examine the thrill of the chase as we seek to capture the criminal. They will also reveal the drama and majesty of the criminal trial as well as the day-to-day reality of a criminal justice system in which trials are the exception and negotiated pleas of guilty are the rule.

When the trial is over or the plea has been entered, when we have separated the innocent from the guilty, the moment of punishment has arrived. The injunction to punish the guilty, to respond to pain inflicted by inflicting pain, is as old as civilization itself. "An eye for an eye and a tooth for a tooth" is a biblical reminder that punishment must measure pain for pain. But our response to the criminal must be better than and different from the crime itself. The biblical admonition, along with the constitutional prohibition of "cruel and unusual punishment," signals that we seek to punish justly and to be just not only in the determination of who can and should be punished, but in how we punish as well. But neither reminder tells us what to do with the wrongdoer. Do we rape the rapist, or burn the home of the arsonist? Surely justice and decency say no. But, if not, then how can and should we punish? In a world in which punishment is neither identical to the crime nor an automatic response to it, choices must be made and we must make them. Books in the CRIME, JUSTICE, AND PUNISHMENT series will examine those choices and the practices, and politics, of punishment. How do we punish and why do we punish as we do? What can we learn about the rationality and appropriateness of today's responses to crime by examining our past and its responses? What works? Is there, and can there be, a just measure of pain?

CRIME, JUSTICE, AND PUNISHMENT brings together books on some of the great themes of human social life. The books in this series capture our fear and fascination with crime and examine our responses to it. They remind us of the deadly seriousness of these subjects. They bring together themes in law, literature, and popular culture to challenge us to think again, to think anew, about subjects that go to the heart of who we are and how we can and will live together.

*   *   *   *   *

Few parts of the criminal justice system are both as significant and yet as little understood as the grand jury. Historically it was thought to be an essential bastion of liberty and a protection against arbitrary abuses of government power. More recently critics say that grand juries have become tools of the government's prosecutorial arm. They point to the fact that grand juries operate in secret; to the absence of constitutional protections, in particular the right to counsel, in grand jury proceedings; and to the ability of grand juries to compel testimony through grants of immunity. In addition, critics note that grand juries rarely refuse to do what prosecutors want. These criticisms as well as the historical role played by grand juries make them an important subject of study.

The Grand Jury provides a much needed, systematic examination of both the past and present of this important institution. This is a well thought-out, well written manuscript. It does a terrific job framing the key issues about the grand jury, telling its history, and providing a compelling contemporary case to frame its presentation. Readers will be swept along by a narrative that skillfully combines argument and example. Examining famous cases, including the Monica Lewinsky case and the Watergate case, as well as the regular practices of the grand jury, this book goes beyond the headlines to show what we gain as well as what we risk in the procedures of grand juries. Finally, by carefully presenting and evaluating several possible reforms, it opens the way for all of us to consider how we might preserve what is valuable while ridding ourselves of the dangers inherent in the grand jury system.

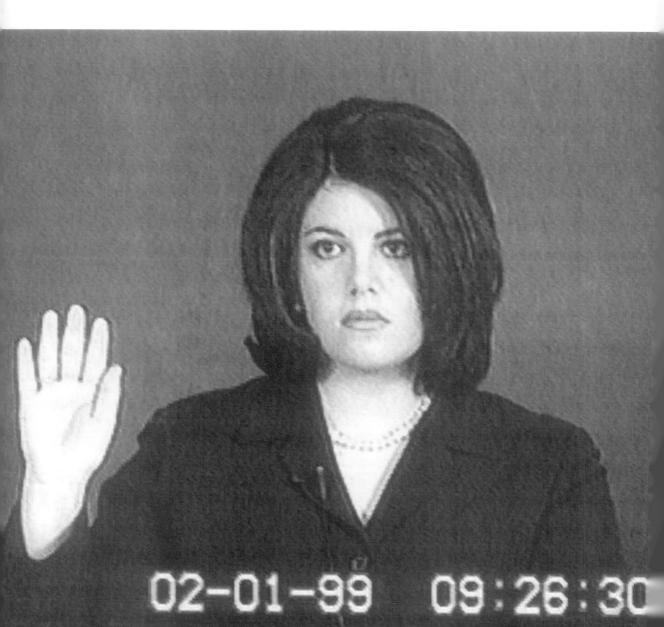

A WOMAN
NAMED MONICA

On January 16, 1998, a young woman was waiting for a friend at a suburban Washington, D.C., shopping mall. She was 24 years old, just a few years out of college, and still wearing her morning workout clothes when she was suddenly confronted by two agents of the Federal Bureau of Investigation (FBI), who ordered her to leave with them. Stunned and frightened, she followed them in an almost trance-like state to a room at the nearby Ritz-Carlton Hotel, where a solemn federal prosecutor proceeded to tell her that if she did not immediately cooperate with their investigation, she could face 27 years in prison.

Room 1012 of the hotel contained not only the prosecutor but a couple of assistants and nine armed agents. For the next 12 hours, they pressured her to talk; urged her to cooperate with the investigation by taping the conversations of other potential witnesses; and threatened her, and her family, with prison. Again and again, the crying young woman begged to speak to a lawyer. Her requests were refused every time. Finally, after her mother had paged her for the third time, the young woman was allowed to call back so that her worried parent wouldn't somehow blow the agents' cover. It was late that night when the young woman's mother finally arrived by train from New York—and with the welcome news that the family had hired an attorney. But the legal nightmare did not stop there.

For nearly a year, the young woman was interrogated repeatedly, asked embarrassing questions about her sex life, and threatened with prison if she did not cooperate. Her weeping mother was forced to testify in court. Her closest friends were also summoned to testify, one from as far away as Japan. Her younger brother was cornered by two FBI agents in his college dorm room. Painful details of her parents' divorce were dredged up from court records and found their way into newspaper stories. Investigators searched her apartment and her personal computer files. They seized love letters she had written but never sent. They even demanded a bookstore's records of what she had bought there.

When her father dared to protest about the treatment of his family, he was told the IRS could come after him for tax evasion and that his medical practice could be probed for Medicare fraud. The resulting media frenzy surrounding the investigation forced the woman to live behind the drawn curtains of her mother's Washington apartment while her weight, the history of her personal relationships, and her deepest insecurities were publicly aired. Legal fees climbed into the hundreds of thousands of dollars, a staggering debt even for her affluent family. The ordeal culminated on August 6, 1998, when the young woman herself finally appeared before a courthouse panel of 23 strangers and was questioned in intimate detail about a recent relationship. As she said later, she felt as though she had been raped.

The young woman, of course, was Monica Lewinsky,

the White House intern whose affair with President Bill Clinton would lead to his historic impeachment by the House of Representatives in January 1999. And the panel of strangers who listened to her story and asked her questions was a grand jury, one of the least understood but most important elements of the criminal justice system.

Most Americans aren't as familiar with the grand jury as they are with trial juries. In fact, when the Lewinsky scandal became public, many news reporters found themselves scrambling to learn about the grand jury system so they could explain it to their audiences. Although many people expressed disdain for the way the Lewinsky story was covered, historians may find that one valuable by-product of the controversy was the way it drew attention to the grand jury system, which has become increasingly obscure in modern times but remains a very powerful institution.

Grand juries are panels of ordinary citizens who, like trial jurors, are summoned to review a criminal case. The difference is that grand juries are impaneled before a case reaches trial and becomes public; the defendant's final guilt or innocence is not for them to decide. Instead, the grand jury's job is determining whether the prosecutor's evidence is strong enough to justify a trial. Thus, a grand jury hearing can be the most important stage of a criminal case, especially a complicated one like the Clinton investigation. A grand jury can deliberate for months while reputations are tarnished, cause innocent bystanders to suffer, and lead eventually to a person's imprisonment. Or, the grand jury can immediately free a target from investigation by declaring the evidence too thin to go on.

If a grand jury decides prosecution is warranted, it returns a written list of charges called an "indictment," or what is more formally known as a "true bill." In a way, an indictment symbolizes a community's seal of approval of police actions and prosecutor accusations.

Independent prosecutor Kenneth W. Starr was the subject of constant media attention as he investigated allegations of wrongdoing by President Clinton. Starr's aggressive tactics, such as the pressure he placed on witnesses like Monica Lewinsky in order to obtain grand jury testimony, were often criticized by observers.

And if the grand jury decides a case should be dropped, it returns a "no bill"—in a sense, a public rejection of the government's case.

Unlike trials, which are open to the public, grand jury proceedings are conducted in private. And, in stark contrast to today's televised trials, court officials take great care to keep the things that go on in grand jury rooms from becoming public. Jurors are sworn to keep all evidence and deliberations secret even after their term of duty ends, and the police and prosecutors are also supposed to keep grand jury matters strictly confidential. One reason for all the secrecy is to protect the reputations of targets and witnesses who come under grand jury scrutiny but are never charged with a crime. Another is to keep accused criminals from fleeing before police have a chance to arrest them. Both reasons make good sense, especially in a society where an accused person is supposed to be considered innocent until proven guilty.

But the grand jury's mantle of secrecy has long been a source of controversy. Secrecy imbues prosecutors with a measure of power that many legal scholars and civil libertarians consider inappropriate in a democracy. In fact, some detractors still derisively refer to grand juries as "star chambers," a term that dates back to the system's origins in medieval England. Back then, jurors were often the handpicked supporters of the king, and they were encouraged to tattle on their neighbors within the privacy of a special room called the Star Chamber. During the Lewinsky controversy, the rather arcane legal phrase became a popular epithet for the Clinton investigation because the prosecutor in charge was named Kenneth W. Starr. Many critics of Starr's aggressive methods, such as the pressure he placed on Lewinsky and her family to discuss Clinton's personal conduct, called his grand jury "the Starr chamber."

Like Starr, the prosecutor in any grand jury proceeding is always the central figure. Only the prosecution presents evidence during this phase of the judicial process, so the prosecutor essentially directs grand jury hearings and greatly influences their outcome. Neither a judge nor the defendant himself is present as the grand jury hears evidence. In fact, in many grand jury proceedings, defense lawyers aren't even allowed in the room while their clients take the witness stand to testify. (Usually, defense lawyers must wait outside and the witnesses must get permission each time they want to leave the grand jury room to consult their attorney— a request that is not automatically granted.) Similarly, the Rules of Evidence that govern trials and help ensure their fairness do not apply to grand jury proceedings. During trials, for example, prosecutors must present any evidence that could clear the defendant. In

Sol Wachtler, the former chief judge of the New York Court of Appeals, was critical of the grand jury system. In 1993, he found himself indicted by a New York grand jury on harassment charges.

grand jury hearings, no such legal obligation exists.

Of course, prosecutors would argue, indicted individuals get a chance to present their side of the story during trial. But the one-sided nature of grand jury proceedings has been a continuing cause for concern. Over time, many state legislatures have abandoned their local grand jury systems in favor of different pre-trial screening methods. California, for example, uses preliminary hearings that are a lot like mini-trials to weed out cases before trial. In New York, county grand juries still review nearly all alleged felonies but a number of reforms—such as allowing witnesses to testify with their lawyers present—have been enacted to make the proceedings more balanced.

There are two basic types of grand juries: the county grand juries that tend to review street crime, and federal grand juries that are drawn from broader geographic districts and hear more complicated matters regulated by federal law. County grand jury proceedings vary from state to state and some states no longer use these grand juries at all. Federal grand juries continue to exist in each of the 50 states and all follow the same set of rules. While county grand juries usually deal with assaults, robberies, murder, and drug possession, federal grand juries tend to hear cases involving tax evasion, white-collar crime, drug trafficking, pollution, and civil rights. Federal grand juries have also been the venue for treason cases and thus hold the greatest potential for political harassment.

Many lawyers and scholars believe that reforms to the federal grand jury system are long overdue. Yet the federal grand jury has remained virtually unchanged since the 18th century when the Founding Fathers, seeking to create protections against malicious prosecution, encoded the right to indictment in the Bill of Rights. That ideal—of the grand jury as a bulwark against government tyranny—seems to have protected it from several repeal movements. Even England, where the grand jury originated in the 12th century, abolished the system in 1933.

In recent times in this country, the grand jury's image as the "people's panel" has been tarnished. In the 20th century, as the nation's legal system has grown more and more complex, prosecutors have gained increasing control over the grand jury process, while jurors themselves have grown more passive. Too often today, grand juries are cynically dismissed as rubber stamps for the prosecution. One of the most famous rebukes of the grand jury system was made in the 1980s by New York State's top judge, Sol Wachtler, who joked that grand juries could be so easily manipulated that, "Any prosecutor who wanted to could indict a ham sandwich." Ironically, Wachtler himself became the "ham" a few years later when a grand jury indicted him

Members of the House Judiciary Committee consider the reams of information about Bill Clinton's alleged misconduct that was collected by Kenneth Starr's grand jury. After reviewing the evidence, the Judiciary Committee recommended that the House of Representatives vote on articles of impeachment. Although four articles of impeachment were passed, Clinton was acquitted of the charges by the Senate.

on charges of harassing a former girlfriend.

Indeed, as the Wachtler and Clinton cases illustrate, grand juries can be used to expose official misconduct. Grand juries not only screen cases against ordinary men but, in theory at least, they are also empowered to investigate wrongdoing among the powerful—by mayors, school board trustees, big business executives, and even the president of the United States. Grand juries are the vehicles used to collect evidence and to summon witnesses to testify, most often through an order to appear in court called a subpoena. Critics argue that grand juries can actually be used to create evidence—by intimidating witnesses into saying what the prosecutor wants. As Lewinsky's situation illustrates, the raw power of the grand jury to subpoena anyone with any scrap of information was one of Starr's main weapons in his investigation of Bill Clinton and his wife, Hillary.

Lewinsky finally agreed to testify, as so many witnesses do, after she was promised that she would not be criminally charged herself. In other words, she was granted immunity from prosecution. Jurors themselves can request more evidence and directly question witnesses, as they did during Lewinsky's testimony and that of Clinton, who became the first sitting president to provide testimony to a grand jury investigating him. Although many Americans questioned the merits of the Starr investigation and Clinton ultimately remained in office, the process nonetheless affirmed that no one is above the law.

But the Starr investigation also illustrated the grand jury's potential for abuse and its effect on the lives of innocent people. Monica Lewinsky was not the first grand jury witness to be harassed and threatened with prison to force her to testify for the prosecution. Nor were she and her mother the first parent and child to be pitted against each other in an effort to squeeze out every drop of potentially damning evidence. Another Starr witness, Susan McDougal, was held in contempt of court and jailed 18 months for refusing to testify against the Clintons, who were old friends. Yet another woman, a minor witness in the scandal named Julie Hiatt Steele, was charged with criminal contempt after she changed her testimony in Clinton's favor and said her original statements were false. The single parent of an adopted child, Steele was threatened with the loss of custody as a result of her peripheral involvement in the case. She also lost her job and became the subject of an Internet website seeking donations to help pay her legal bills.

The grand jurors who heard Monica Lewinsky's testimony apparently sympathized with her. "Here is a young woman who could be any one of us," grand jury forewoman Freda Alexander later commented.

Still another flaw in the grand jury system that can damage innocent bystanders—leaks of information despite secrecy rules—plagued the Starr investigation. One news story after another detailed Starr's strategy and his negotiations with Lewinsky's lawyers over immunity. How did this confidential material reach reporters? Starr's top spokesman finally resigned amid suspicions that most of the leaked information was coming from the prosecutor's staff. And Starr himself became the subject of a Department of Justice investigation into alleged ethics violations.

All these facets have prompted legal experts to ask: Is the grand jury system still the "people's panel" envisioned by the Founding Fathers? Is it really just a rubber stamp for prosecutors? Has the shield against tyranny actually become an instrument of oppression? Has the grand jury outgrown its function as a government watchdog? Should it be abolished, or somehow changed?

Lewinsky's own account of her experience seems to suggest that grand jurors can still fulfill their role as ordinary people applying common sense to even the most complex of government cases. During her grueling testimony, for example, the entire grand jury wept as Lewinsky described her detention in the Ritz-Carlton Hotel. One grand juror who had been especially hostile toward Lewinsky finally told her she forgave her affair with a married man. Several others urged Lewinsky, as she wrapped up her testimony, to move on with her life. The forewoman moved Lewinsky to tears by telling her: "We wanted to offer you a bouquet of good wishes that includes luck, success, happiness and blessings." In a subsequent interview with the *New York Times*, forewoman Freda Alexander said she herself had sympathized with everyone involved in the case, including Clinton, Starr, and especially Lewinsky. "Here is a young woman who could be any one of us if we were to truly admit it," Alexander said. "I don't think she's a hussy. I think she's a young person full of enthusiasm, willing to try new things."

If nothing else, the Starr investigation demonstrated what a mixed bag the grand jury can be, a fascinating sword of justice that is indeed double-edged.

THE NUTS AND BOLTS

A jury is sworn in before hearing testimony. Grand juries are most common in New York City; nearly every criminal case is reviewed by a grand jury to determine whether or not it should go to trial. About 25,000 people serve on New York State grand juries each year.

Every weekday at 10 A.M. and 2 P.M., grand jurors in the heart of New York City report to one of several court buildings on Centre Street, near the City Hall complex and New York Police Department headquarters. Most likely they take the subway, exit at the Franklin Street or Chambers Street stops, and walk along Lower Manhattan's narrow sidewalks past corner delis and diners, nail salons, and immigrant vendors selling all manner of hats, gloves, scarves, and trinkets. Once settled inside one of the Manhattan Supreme Court's nine grand jury rooms, far from the din of traffic and never-ending construction work, jurors are enveloped in quiet and secrecy—a seeming miracle in the nation's most densely populated metropolis. Yet the cases they hear and the diversity of their members reflect the urban world around them, just as the country's first grand juries in the colony of Massachusetts mirrored the world of the Puritans.

New York obviously has one of the busiest court systems in the country, and its state and county grand juries are surely the most active. They are also unusual, not only because of the sheer volume of criminal cases they review but because they review them at all; only about a dozen states in the country still rely on local grand juries to examine routine street crimes. New York's grand jury system makes a good case study because of this. Its complexity and expense also demonstrate why other states have chosen alternative methods for weeding out cases before trial.

In Manhattan, one of the city's five boroughs, there are 13 separate grand juries hearing cases every Monday through Friday. (Brooklyn, Queens, Staten Island, and the Bronx, New York City's four other boroughs, each maintain their own grand juries.) During the course of a year throughout New York State, a whopping 25,000 people will be sworn in to review the parade of alleged crimes. In Manhattan, to make the job less of a burden, they work in split shifts—from 10 A.M. until 1 P.M. and from 2 until 5 P.M.—a fairly recent change aimed at making the public more willing to serve.

Twenty-three people are impaneled for each grand jury with the assumption there will be absences during the course of its term. A quorum of 16 panelists is needed to hear evidence, and a minimum vote of 12 is required for an indictment. Most grand juries are convened for four weeks under New York State's current system. A few so-called special grand juries are impaneled to hear extraordinary matters involving organized crime, Medicare and Medicaid fraud, investment fraud, and occasionally, official corruption. Special grand juries often sit for longer terms than the standard four weeks and can tie up their jurors for months.

But it is the regular, county grand juries that hear the meat and potatoes of crime—the arrests for drug possession, wife beating, burglary, and even murders whose circumstances have become so common in a big city they never find their way into the newspaper.

Let's say city police catch a person strolling through Central Park smoking a joint. When this person is searched, police find more marijuana and some cocaine in his pockets—felony drug possession under the New York State criminal code. Here's what would happen: The person would be placed under arrest and taken down to the police station for a process known as "booking," in which he is fingerprinted, photographed, and officially entered into law-enforcement records. (This is what the cops in the movies or TV are referring to when they growl, "Book him!") After several hours in jail (ideally no more than 24 hours) the person will be "arraigned," or brought before a judge in a court-room to formally hear the accusations against him. If the judge decides to keep the accused person in jail, within six days a grand jury must hear the evidence and decide whether or not to indict the accused person. That deadline is intended to protect the defendant's right against being detained without probable cause. If the judge releases the accused on bail, the police and prosecutors have six months to bring the case before a grand jury, a deadline designed to protect the defendant's right to a speedy trial. Either way, the accused person will return to court to appear again before a judge and learn the grand jury's decision.

When the case finally comes before the grand jury, it will likely unfold in a dingy room with hard, wooden benches, a sour smell, and not a single picture on the walls. The prosecutor will control the entire process—calling the witnesses, asking the questions, introducing any physical evidence in his effort to persuade the grand jurors to indict, or give their blessing to the charges against, the accused person.

There is no judge present to protect the rights of both sides, as in trials. And unlike trials, which these days are often broadcast on cable TV, the public is strictly barred from grand jury proceedings. The secrecy is meant to protect witnesses and targets from being unfairly tainted by the investigation, an echo of the basic tenet that one is innocent until proven guilty. Secrecy also enables the police to arrest an accused criminal before he or she can escape. But it also provides law-enforcement authorities with a shield against being scrutinized themselves, and allows for plenty of discretion on the part of the prosecutor. The only other people in the room, besides the grand jurors, are a stenographer and an armed warden.

New York State allows defendants the option of testifying before the grand jury, and also allows their defense lawyers to be present in the grand jury room during that testimony. In contrast to trials, however, the defense lawyers may not argue with the prosecutor, address the grand jury directly, or cross-examine witnesses. The largely silent defense lawyer is there mainly to prepare for his client's presumed future trial and keep the defendant from self-incrimination. This differs from the rules for federal grand juries, which are extremely controversial. Defense lawyers may not be present at all in the federal grand jury room. If witnesses want to consult their lawyers while testifying, they must have the presence of mind and the courage to interrupt the proceedings and ask the prosecutor's permission to leave the room. And permission is not always granted. Defense lawyer Gerald Lefcourt recalled a case in which his client, the wife of a drug-investigation target, invoked her right to remain silent only to have the prosecutor berate her and shout at her in an effort to wear her down as a witness. (The law recognizes marriage as a "privileged" relationship, so spouses have the right to remain silent to avoid incriminating their husbands or wives.) The wife's repeated requests to consult her

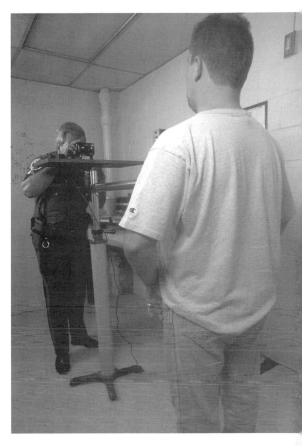

lawyer were ignored. The prosecutor's voice was so loud, Lefcourt said, he could hear it in the hallway. He said he had to pound on the grand jury room door to stop the proceedings, then go before a judge to insist that the prosecutor's abuse be stopped.

One recent county grand juror in Manhattan, a 27-year-old newspaper reporter who was born and raised in the city, noted that almost each time a defendant did take the stand, the grand jury either did not issue an indictment or indicted the accused on a lesser charge. That was because the defendants often seemed to have reasonable rebuttals to the prosecutor's evidence. In one case, the reporter explained, a clean-cut Asian medical student from Long Island claimed he had been harassed and held up for money by a black man outside

After the suspect in a criminal investigation has been fingerprinted and photographed, he or she is brought before a judge to hear the charges. In New York State, a grand jury must review the case within six days if the judge decides to keep the suspect in jail. If the suspect is allowed free on bail, prosecutors have six months to present their case to the grand jury.

Central Park. The next day, the accused testified and told the grand jury he was HIV-positive, a drug user, and an occasional male prostitute who had been selling the other man sex when they began arguing over money. "The cops favored the account of the well-dressed Asian guy over the semi-homeless black guy and arrested him," the grand juror recalled later. "When you heard the one side it was like an open-and-shut mugging. When you heard the other side it was, like, 'Wow. The story was entirely different.'"

In this particular grand juror's opinion, the alleged mugging case underscored how one-sided and unfair the whole grand jury system can be. "It's a terrifying process," the journalist said of his grand jury experience. "Once you're caught in that machinery I imagine it would be a terrifying thing because it is so easy to charge and indict someone." Courthouse veterans say it is rare for a defendant to testify before the grand jury; indeed, defendants took the witness stand only four or five times during the young journalist's month on the grand jury. Those who do testify represent the few with plausible defenses; the majority keep their mouths shut for fear of digging themselves in deeper with lies and inconsistencies. During a trial, a prosecutor can introduce a defendant's grand jury testimony to impeach his credibility on the witness stand. So most defendants choose not to address the grand jury. When one does, courthouse veterans have observed, it seems to have a favorable psychological effect on grand jurors, who often equate that testimony with innocence.

Regardless of whether the defendant testifies, most cases are presented within 20 minutes or less, making for a mind-numbing experience that leaves little time or energy to raise doubts. Although in theory, New York's grand jurors are empowered to initiate their own investigations and call their own witnesses, veterans of the system acknowledge they rarely do. The young journalist interviewed for this book said he raised several questions during the course of his term—but all had to be funneled through the prosecutor, who then asked the question directly in front of the grand jurors.

Occasionally, the courthouse tedium can be interrupted by a celebrity case—or a tragedy. During the young reporter's recent tour of duty, a convicted crack dealer jumped to his death from the 13th floor rather than face prison. His body literally fell past the window of the grand jury room as an assistant district attorney was wrapping up a presentation. "People sort of looked at each other and then someone later told me I said out loud, 'Was that a body?'" the journalist recalled. It was a horrifying event, and a court administrator told the grand jurors that anyone who wanted to be excused from service, would be. Still, the grand jury resumed the next day, as did the rest of the court's business.

In 1998, 11,653 indictments—92 percent of the cases presented—were returned by Manhattan grand juries. This statistic seems to support critics' claims that the grand jury is little more than a rubber stamp for the prosecution. The majority of these cases are resolved through plea agreements; fewer than 10 percent actually get to trial, and of those, the Manhattan District Attorney's Office claims a conviction rate of 75 to 80 percent. However, New York also gives indicted defendants the right to have a judge review the grand jury transcripts. Some cases are dismissed as a result of these reviews, which can turn up errors by the prosecution or prompt a judge to conclude that the evidence was weak.

Vincent J. Homenick, a lifelong civil servant in Manhattan Supreme Court who is chief clerk of the jury division, is among the growing number of people who feel grand juries may no longer be necessary. It costs the Manhattan Supreme Court system about $15 million a year to impanel and maintain all its juries—trial juries as well as grand juries. That figure includes the cost of sequestering trial jurors deliberating over high-profile cases and the $40-per-day stipend

Grand jury hearings are opportunities for prosecutors to present their cases without rebuttals or additional evidence from defense attorneys. Some critics of the grand jury system feel that these citizen review panels are too dependent on information from prosecutors, and simply approve law-enforcement officials' cases without weighing all the evidence available.

available to all jurors. Despite these practical concerns, which are a big part of his job, Homenick has an interesting theory about the enduring appeal of the grand jury. In the view of this friendly and efficient court administrator, the aura of mystery surrounding the grand jury and the consensus of 12 people to indict, in writing, is an extremely powerful symbol of the law. "It's moving when the clerk reads you've been indicted by a New York grand jury," Homenick said.

The state of California dispensed with such symbolism more than 20 years ago, replacing the grand jury hearing in criminal cases with a process known as a probable cause hearing. In this so-called "mini-trial," a judge, rather than a panel of laymen, hears a sampling of the evidence and decides whether the matter deserves a full trial. Using legal language reminiscent of England's early grand juries, California prosecutors present their cases based on information they have received from the police or their own investigators. In probable cause hearings, defense lawyers are not only present, they can make legal arguments before the judge and cross-examine the prosecution's witnesses. (The defense does not present its own case during these hearings.) Probable cause hearings take place at the municipal court level (usually the venue for misdemeanors), even if the cases involve felonies. A famous example is the 1994 murder case involving O. J. Simpson, whose one-week mini-trial in Los Angeles Municipal Court drew more attention than most full trials. If a judge decides the charges are worth pursuing, as the judge did in the Simpson affair, then the case is "bound over" to the superior court level for trial.

The California Supreme Court mandated the use of probable cause hearings in 1978 after finding that a defendant charged by indictment was "seriously disadvantaged in contrast to a defendant charged by information." The following year, the Wisconsin legislature enacted the terms of the California ruling and also began using probable cause hearings instead of grand juries. Both states allow prosecutors the option of seeking a grand jury indictment but even when they do, a two-sided probable cause hearing must be held. Why would a prosecutor bother with the grand jury at all in these states? Sometimes, cases involving several defendants and complex paper trails can be too cumbersome for probable cause hearings and a grand jury can be a helpful investigative tool. Sometimes, in extremely volatile cases, prosecutors make use of the grand jury's secrecy to avoid a spectacle before trial.

And sometimes, prosecutors who believe a case is weak but are under political pressure to bring charges will use a grand jury to return a no bill rather than saying so themselves. In the puzzling JonBenet Ramsay murder case in Colorado, for example, many observers believed that was why the prosecutor went before a grand jury: because an outraged public wanted to see someone, anyone, stand trial for the killing of a six-year-old beauty queen, but there was not enough solid evidence to charge anyone. In New York, one former federal prosecutor recalled a case that he considered bogus but was under pressure to pursue because it involved a fellow federal employee. A white female Secret Service agent had been jostled on a subway train by two black riders. She wasn't hurt, but was so angry and humiliated that she wanted them charged under federal law with assaulting an agent. Although the prosecutor felt such a charge was unwarranted, he dutifully presented the facts to a grand jury. Yet his voice and body language somehow conveyed his views and a no bill was returned. "I wanted the grand jury to understand this was a case that warranted extra listening to," he acknowledged.

Although California grand juries no longer hear most criminal cases, the state still uses county grand juries to review the workings of government. These panels set their own agendas, sit for a year, and tend to include jurors who are retired or unemployed (who else has the time?). Their reports are useful but, unfortunately, action is often not taken on the official findings.

An example of this occurred in 1997, when a Marin County, California, grand jury released its investigation into the educational quality of a local school district. Following up on numerous complaints about the Sausalito School System, located just north of San Francisco, the grand jurors found that even though the district's average class size was 18 students and the average spending per student was $12,276 per year (nearly three times the average of other schools in Marin County), student performance in Sausalito elementary schools was far below average. The grand jury report concluded that district leadership was lacking, teacher morale was low, and a lack of student discipline contributed to the decline in education in Sausalito. As a result, district taxpayers were receiving a poor return for their investment. However, although the Marin County report caused headlines, it did not lead to immediate changes in the school district.

State and local grand juries were abolished as early as 1859 in Michigan, whose lawmakers decided they were too much like "star chambers," the secretive fishing expeditions conducted against citizens behind closed doors in medieval England. Instead, the Michigan legislature provided that all crimes be prosecuted on information rather than indictment, and that only a judge could convene a grand jury for purposes of a special investigation. Michigan's action reflected the concerns of the mid-1800s as the country continued to expand. As new states were holding constitutional conventions, legislators debated whether the right to grand jury indictment was "an essential bulwark of liberty" or a "remnant of the barbaric past."

Grand jury indictments were not commonly used in Pennsylvania until the 1970s because of such deep-seated skepticism; before 1975, when state law changed, prosecutors had to petition the court each time they wanted to convene a grand jury. Even then, the list of charges they wanted grand jurors to review had to be tightly drafted. The Hawaii legislature recently appointed legal advisors for grand juries to help preserve their independence from prosecutors. And North Carolina has a unique system in which prosecutors aren't even allowed in the grand jury room. Only witnesses and the grand jurors themselves are present, and the proceedings are not recorded.

In contrast to the variety of local justice systems, federal grand juries continue to meet regularly in each of the 50 states and they all follow the same rules under the management of the U.S. Department of Justice. They are drawn from the local populace, as are state and county grand juries, but federal grand juries follow slightly different procedures and tend to hear more complicated cases. Their main function is to investigate federal offenses such as civil rights violations, environmental abuses, fraud, and, increasingly, drug

One of the functions of the grand jury is to act as a "people's panel," protecting ordinary citizens from abuses by those in power. A grand jury indicted these four New York police officers (clockwise from top left: Justin Volpe, Thomas Bruder, Thomas Wiese and Charles Schwarz) for their brutal attack on Abner Louima, a Haitian immigrant.

trafficking. And, as Americans saw in both the Clinton investigation and in the Watergate investigation into the administration of President Richard Nixon 25 years earlier, it is federal grand juries that review charges of misconduct by high-level government officials—even sitting Presidents.

Often, federal grand juries provide a cleanup function after cases fail at the local level. In the 1991 police beating of Rodney G. King, for example, it was a federal grand jury in Los Angeles that indicted four white police officers on charges of violating the black motorist's civil rights. King had been driving erratically on a Los Angeles freeway when he was stopped by patrol officers, who beat him into submission. What the police did not realize was that a neighbor was standing on his apartment balcony trying out his new video camera. He taped the entire incident. The videotape, which plainly showed officers repeatedly kicking and hitting King with clubs while others watched, caused an uproar when it aired nationally. Yet the four alleged ringleaders were acquitted of assault charges after a long trial in county court. So federal prosecutors tried again, this time pressing civil-rights charges and finally winning the officers' convictions in U.S. District Court in Los Angeles.

Federal grand juries usually meet in nicer surroundings and have access to more sophisticated expert witnesses than local grand juries, thanks to the bigger budget of the U.S. Attorney's Office. But because they are also controlled by the prosecutor, federal grand juries are criticized as "rubber stamp justice." One former federal grand juror observed that in every case in which indictment was sought by the federal prosecutor, it was delivered—and almost always unanimously. Blanche Davis Blank left her two-year tenure on a federal grand jury extremely critical of the one-sided process.

"The formal and somewhat austere atmosphere of the grand jury room is probably consciously designed to intimidate witnesses," Blank wrote in her book *The Not So Grand Jury: The Story of the Federal Grand Jury System*. "The entire procedure is really a prosecutor's chance at a free-wheeling dress rehearsal. A wide range of questions can be asked—a broad net cast to see what might be reeled in."

But the former federal prosecutor who handled the Secret Service agent's case took a more pragmatic view. "The grand jury is not there to provide a bulwark," he said. "It is a simple machine for evaluating simple evidence. It only rises to a historic role when the parties involved push the right buttons."

EYE OF THE BEHOLDER

In the legal system of the United States, justice is supposed to treat all citizens equally, regardless of their race, gender, or background. However, grand jury decisions can vary significantly, depending on the feelings and beliefs of the people serving on these panels.

T he scene was a Manhattan grand jury room and a panel of strangers, on its very first day of duty, was deliberating over a seemingly routine mugging. An accused thief had been arrested for holding up a cab driver along with an armed partner who had gotten away. The grand jury was deciding whether to indict the defendant on a set of charges including attempted robbery and assault.

The cabbie, a recent immigrant from Africa, testified through an interpreter in his native Fulani. He said one man had aimed a gun through the cab's window and the defendant, already in the back seat of the car, had grabbed him around the neck. He said he managed to push down the armed man outside the cab, floored the accelerator and sped towards the nearest police station. The thief in the back seat started to beat him, then fled, before being quickly arrested. But the defendant offered a different version of events: he claimed the cab driver "just flipped out," sped off with him, and attacked him before he managed to escape. The defendant's testimony "was completely not plausible in my view," recalled the young journalist on the panel.

Yet in the end, the journalist was among the minority believing the defendant deserved to be indicted; the grand jury actually acquitted the defendant of two of three charges. A majority seemed to sympathize with the accused's claims of a misunderstanding with a foreigner. Like many big city residents, they themselves had had frustrating encounters with immigrant cab drivers. One woman in particular, the journalist recalled, remarked: "I know these cab drivers. They need to learn to speak English." Clearly, her personal experience affected her perspective on this case.

Prosecutors undoubtedly control grand jury hearings but history has repeatedly shown that the type of people sitting on any jury can make all the difference in its actions. Race, religion, class, education, political beliefs, and life experience inevitably influence any juror's decision, no matter how skilled the prosecutor or how strong his case. A balanced panel of jurors seems imperative, but this is not so easy to achieve. For centuries, grand juries were made up mainly of white men who had the property and connections to get appointed to duty. That is no longer the case; grand jurors are now selected randomly. However, impaneling diverse grand juries is hardly problem free. Today, the most pressing issue seems to be getting citizens simply to serve—to set aside their cynicism and temporarily leave behind jobs, schooling, children, and daily routines to take part in the workings of justice.

King Henry II, the ruler of England from 1154 to 1189, recognized the importance of juror selection when he created the grand jury system. Because the panels of citizens were designed to enhance his power against that of the church, jurors were handpicked either by the king himself or his nobles to ensure that the crown's business and policies were enforced throughout the land. In the 1600s, when the Catholic king Charles II sought treason charges against the Protestant leaders Stephen Colledge and the earl of Shaftesbury, the king moved the matter from London to Oxford, where he had more supporters. In London, a panel of sympathetic Protestants had refused to indict Colledge and Shaftesbury in the first recorded instance of grand jury mutiny.

Location remains a key factor in criminal cases today, as the 1991 Rodney King beating in Los Angeles illustrates so well. In that case, four white officers in the Los Angeles Police Department were charged with assaulting King, a black motorist initially stopped for driving erratically. Their defense lawyers, arguing that pretrial publicity made it impossible to find impartial jurors in LA, succeeded in moving the trial out of Los Angeles. Instead, it took place in suburban Simi Valley, a politically conservative town known for the large number of police officers who lived there. The resulting trial jury acquitted the four officers, a verdict that sparked the 1992 Los Angeles riots. Outraged blacks and Latinos said the King case was just one more example of how police mistreated minorities and managed to avoid punishment. Later, after a federal grand jury indicted the officers on a different set of charges, a racially diverse trial jury drawn from metropolitan Los Angeles convicted the officers of violating King's civil rights.

The racial tensions of the King case echoed the countervailing actions of grand juries in the North and South around the time of the Civil War. Grand jurors in the antebellum South often used their power to enforce slavery laws and guard against insurrection. They indicted liberal masters who taught their slaves to read, or allowed them such freedoms as traveling by horse and buggy or congregating without a white escort. Southern grand jurors also indicted bartenders and others who sold whiskey to slaves. As the abolitionist

Standing behind photos of the four Los Angeles Police Department officers accused of beating African-American motorist Rodney King, Los Angeles district attorney Ira Reiner discusses the King case with the media. The subsequent trial of the police officers shows how location can affect a jury's decision: the local jury, drawn not from Los Angeles but from a nearby mostly-white suburb, acquitted the four officers. The case also shows the grand jury system working to protect citizens like King: a federal grand jury was impaneled after the King verdict, and the four police officers were indicted and eventually convicted of civil rights violations.

movement gained momentum, grand juries in the South indicted outspoken ministers who advocated ending slavery and the "Underground Railroad" smugglers who helped slaves to freedom across the Mason-Dixon line. In addition to indictments, Southern grand juries issued many recommendations on the subject of slavery. One Maryland panel offered the unconstitutional suggestion that the postmaster screen all "inflammatory" abolitionist literature sent through the mail.

In the North, meanwhile, grand juries addressed the increasing problem of freed and runaway slaves being kidnapped and returned to the South in exchange for handsome rewards. Abolitionist sympathies ran so high that a Syracuse grand jury indicted a federal marshal who had arrested a fugitive slave in the line of duty. Northern grand juries also reflected the tensions between local whites and unemployed, recently freed slaves living side-by-side: One Philadelphia grand jury in 1823 recommended banning "free Negroes" from the city because of the dance halls and bars cropping up in their neighborhoods. And after riots broke out following an 1842 demonstration by blacks celebrating the end of slavery in the West Indies, another Philadelphia grand jury blamed the community of freed slaves for "undue provocation." In the border states, where treason arrests were rampant, divided loyalties became such a concern that a Kentucky senator introduced a bill requiring grand jurors to swear they had never aided the South. Congress enacted the measure in 1862.

During the post–Civil War period known as Reconstruction, grand jury indictments became ammunition in the political battle between southern Democrats (the more traditional party dominated by whites) and Radicals (who favored liberal rights for blacks and often included freed slaves). In 1868 in Dallas County, Alabama, for example, almost every Radical official was under indictment by an all-white grand jury. The same year, a Democratic grand jury's indictment of a black state senator from Leon County, Florida, on bribery charges sparked accusations that his case was racially motivated. Predictably, whoever controlled the sheriff's office—Democrats or Radicals—controlled the selection of grand jurors and determined whether blacks would be impaneled. Each party accused the other of election fraud as blacks began voting for the first time.

As the modern-day Rodney King case reminds us, federal and local juries often arrive at vastly different conclusions about the same event. Federal grand juries are drawn from broader geographic areas than county grand juries, making for a more diverse pool of panelists. Federal prosecutors, meanwhile, often have very different agendas than county prosecutors beholden to local voters.

In Lexington, Kentucky, a county grand jury and a federal grand jury simultaneously investigated an 1871 election-day riot in which three blacks were killed and many others were injured. The Fayette County grand jury said it was unable to discover who was to blame for the riot. However, the federal grand jury indicted six people, including several city officials and officers of the state militia, whom they accused of first provoking voters and then using excessive force to quell the violence.

In the years after the Civil War when a racist hate group called the Ku Klux Klan began terrorizing blacks in the South, grand juries consistently refused to indict KKK members—often for fear of retribution. Congress finally enacted the sweeping Ku Klux Klan Act of 1871, which made it a federal crime to conspire against someone's civil rights. The highly controversial measure authorized the use of federal troops to protect the rights of blacks to vote and also broadened the jurisdiction of federal grand juries so they could address the problem. The federal grand juries were carefully screened and often omitted whites. The juries began indicting Klan members and their supporters so liberally that by the end of 1873, more than 1,300 cases crowded the dockets of federal courts throughout the South.

The partisan nature—and subtle power—of grand juries was also evident in Utah Territory in the 1850s. Mormon-dominated grand juries refused to indict fellow church members either for polygamy (a marriage where a spouse can have more than one mate at a time—for example, a man with three wives) or for violently resisting non-Mormon settlers. Conversely, the grand jurors found grounds to indict critics of their church. Once again, the actions of the grand jury reflected a broader political struggle: the Mormon settlers of Utah wanted to join the ever-growing list of states, but the federal government first wanted the Mormons to change some aspects of their religion, such as polygamy.

One way Mormon officials asserted their independence was by establishing church-led probate courts in each county and empowering the judges to name all grand jurors, including federal grand jurors. Like King Henry II, the Mormon leaders realized that power lay in controlling who was indicted and who was not. One non-Mormon judge who refused to recognize the probate courts and who was critical of Mormon beliefs was himself indicted for "assault and battery with intent to murder" after a street scuffle. When Judge W. W. Drummond responded by trying to get another grand jury to charge church leaders with polygamy, the grand jurors

A Ku Klux Klan leader reads a story in his local newspaper about his appearance before a grand jury probe of alleged KKK activities. In the post–Reconstruction South, the decisions of local and federal grand juries often reflected their racial makeup: the local juries, usually composed of white citizens, turned a blind eye to racial violence, while the racially diverse federal grand juries attacked groups like the KKK that committed hate crimes against African Americans.

refused to return any indictments. Drummond was forced to resign and left for California.

The Drummond affair influenced President James Buchanan's decision to send federal troops into Salt Lake City in the summer of 1857, a measure that forced the Mormon leader Brigham Young to step down as governor and that helped escalate mistrust of federal authority in the territory. About the same time, the federal government was trying to prosecute the so-called Mountain Meadows Massacre of 1857, in which Mormon leaders were being blamed for the mass murder of 140 non-Mormon settlers on their way from Arkansas to California. Grand jurors refused to cooperate in issuing any indictments. The frustrated federal judge on the case had little choice but to close his court and release the defendants. In fact, federal authority triumphed in Utah only after Congress's Poland Act of 1874, which barred polygamists from serving on grand juries hearing such cases and shifted jury selection to federal court officials. Utah joined the Union in 1896, becoming the 45th state.

Although in recent years, jury duty of any kind has been widely regarded as a dreaded task to be avoided at all cost, grand juries were long considered an elite group. Their members joined alumni associations, held socials, and influenced the selection of new grand juries by nominating friends and colleagues to the county clerk or sheriff. Obviously, this was an exclusive, self-perpetuating system that often resembled a country club. Yet admirers of the method say the quality of the grand jurors was always high, with self-confident, well-educated pillars of the community making wise judges of evidence. Sometimes they became fearless pursuers of evidence, too. "The grand jury associations in New York were always very civic-minded," said Norman Goodman, the affable county clerk of New York County (Manhattan). "They were very well thought of and sort of oversaw mores in the city."

In 1968, Congress dramatically changed the composition of all grand juries with the Jury Selection and Service Act. The measure opened up the traditionally all-white, all-male panels by barring exclusion on the basis of age, race, religion, gender, national origin, or economic status. However, New York relied on the so-called key man system until 1975, when the state legislature required that jurors be randomly selected from the rolls of registered voters. At the same time, New York repealed a state law that had exempted women from duty (based on the idea that they were the main caretakers of children). New York's action followed a decision by the U.S. Supreme Court in a matter known as *Taylor v. Louisiana*. The landmark case challenged Louisiana's tradition of refusing to subpoena women to grand jury duty (although, in theory, women could volunteer for grand jury duty at their parish seat). The Supreme Court found that grand juries had to be "fair and representative cross-sections" of society, a ruling that triggered the use of random selection nationwide.

New York has since broadened its pool of prospective jurors beyond registered voters, who represent only about two-thirds of eligible adults and continue to include a disproportionate number of whites. Today the state's computers also scan the lists of registered drivers, state income tax payers, welfare recipients, and those receiving unemployment compensation to enlist anyone over the age of 18. (Convicted felons are not eligible to serve.)

The system was refined even further in 1996 when the state legislature, in an effort to create an even greater mix of jurors, repealed all occupational exemptions—rules that had allowed the members of some professions to avoid grand jury duty. In the previous two decades, New York's juries had become increasingly dominated by schoolteachers, blue-collar workers, government workers, the unemployed, and retirees. It was unheard of for a doctor, lawyer, engineer, or business

Jurors line up outside the Queens (New York) County Courthouse. Getting people from all walks of life to serve their communities on grand juries can be problematic; New York and other municipalities have instituted reforms to make it easier for anyone to serve.

executive to take the time out to serve. That was because, frankly, jury duty can be disruptive and tedious. Federal grand juries, for example, are drawn from such a large geographic area that some panelists must commute several hours round-trip to the nearest U.S. district courthouse. Complicated cases can last weeks, even months. Jury duty can mean a loss of income because many employers will not pay workers on extended leaves. Government employees continue to be paid during jury duty, which explains the high number of teachers and bureaucrats who serve. For those whose regular paycheck will stop during jury duty,

New York pays $40 a day, a stipend that hardly equals most salaries but will cover the costs of transportation and lunch. But many jurisdictions pay less; Los Angeles offers jurors only $5 a day, an amount that won't even cover parking costs in that car-dependent city.

The net effect was that lower-paid, less-educated people, or government workers less inclined to challenge prosecutors, were bearing the brunt of jury duty. That led to more passive and gullible panels, some critics say, and also promoted the rather un-American impression that the privileged didn't have to serve. In one infamous New York case, a cocky young vice president of a Wall Street brokerage house tried to get his auto mechanic to serve in his place! He was caught, sentenced to 100 hours of community service, and by all accounts made an exemplary (and very contrite) temporary clerk at Manhattan Supreme Court.

Today in New York, ditch diggers serve alongside celebrities thanks to a number of reforms, including Manhattan's use of half-day shifts. The office of jury manager Vincent Homenick is adorned with the autographed photos of Katie Couric, Bernadette Peters, Ed Bradley, Tom Brokaw, and Marisa Tomei, among other familiar faces, all of whom have served on either trial or grand juries. "You really know how to show a girl a good time," actress Tomei wrote on her photograph. The court hosts a "jurors appreciation day" once a year, passes out commemorative mugs, and asks its celebrity alumni to help spread the word that jury duty is for everyone.

A HISTORY OF CONTROVERSY

The bitter legal and political disputes associated with the Kenneth Starr grand jury are hardly new. Since its inception in England in the 12th century, the grand jury system has often been a battleground between warring political factions, with the threat of criminal charges and jail a potent weapon against enemies. In this country, whether hearing routine cases or ones destined to make history, grand juries have also proven to be uncanny reflections of their communities and their times.

King Henry II, known as the founder of the English system of common law, created the grand jury as part of an effort to wrest power away from the Roman Catholic Church. At the time, ecclesiastical (or church-supervised) courts governed everyday matters such as marriages, wills, and property rights. Ecclesiastical courts also prosecuted a range of crimes, including murder, usually on the basis of accusations brought by equally powerful land barons.

King Henry II (1133–89) of England created the grand jury system in order to shift power from the Catholic Church to the state.

51

For about 500 years, grand juries in England were filled with people who would do as their king ordered. The first incidence of a grand jury that rebelled against the king's wishes occurred in 1660, under England's King Charles II (1630–85). However, the king merely dismissed the jury and impaneled a new one that would provide the indictments he sought.

In 1164 the Church agreed to recognize panels of local citizens, forerunners of today's grand juries, which would screen criminal accusations. New laws established under Henry II said a bishop's accusations in court could not be based on undisclosed sources. If an informant did not want to go public with his complaint, the new laws said, then the local sheriff of each shire, or county, would appoint two dozen men to hear the evidence against the alleged offender and decide whether any charges deserved to be presented in court. A quorum of 16 jurors was needed to hear the evidence and 12 votes were required for an indictment, or formal set of criminal charges. Indictments were also known as "true bills" when they resulted from charges sought by the king and "presentments" when they were generated by the grand jurors themselves, based on their own knowledge of events in their towns.

From a human rights standpoint, the new laws were remarkably progressive; before, privately brought charges forced accused criminals to find 11 men willing to swear to their innocence—an unlikely prospect in the face of a bishop's power. For the first time, in theory at least, the new system of review introduced the notion that an accused man just might be innocent and ought to be viewed that way until proven guilty.

But Henry II's motives weren't entirely idealistic. For one thing, the Church's courts had been reaping significant revenues in fines and the king coveted that source of income. The grand jurors themselves became potential sources of revenue for the king because heavy fines were levied on those who failed to respond to a summons to serve—or who failed to return an indictment. The new panels of appointed, carefully screened

men also strengthened the king's control over his subjects because grand jurors were expected to turn in suspected criminals from among their relatives, neighbors,
and acquaintances. So although grand juries had the
potential to buffer ordinary men from criminal charges,
they in fact proved themselves to be citizen police
forces that had little choice but to carry out the will of
the king.

The unquestioned authority of the panels as exten-
sions of the king remained unchallenged for some 500
years. But during the 1600s, when Parliament evolved
into an independent branch of government with the
power of taxation, the importance of the grand jury as
a royal revenue source was greatly diminished. The
17th century also saw another important development
in the course of the grand jury that once again stemmed
from England's tension between church and state. By
then, the Protestant Anglican Church was the domi-
nant religious force in England and a dissident King
Charles II, a member of the House of Stuart, was trying
to reestablish the Roman Catholic Church. When
Charles sought treason charges against two prominent
Protestants who opposed his campaign, Anthony Ash-
ley Cooper, the earl of Shaftesbury, and Stephen
Colledge, a grand jury comprised mainly of Protestants
defied the king and refused to return indictments
against them. The 1681 denial of a true bill became the
first recorded act of independence by a grand jury.
Although the king simply appointed a new grand jury
willing to do his bidding, and Shaftesbury and Colledge
were eventually arrested and executed, the stage was set
for grand juries to express the will of the people.

That's what happened in colonial America, where
grand juries would become important weapons in the
revolt against British rule. English settlers brought the
grand jury system with them to the New World and the
panels quickly developed into feisty agencies that not
only monitored the behavior of common men but also

watched over the actions of local officials who represented the English king. The first regular grand jury sat in Massachusetts in 1635. It not only charged colony residents with such standard offenses as wife beating but also initiated inquests against local trustees. In the town of Sandwich, for example, various officials were rebuked by the grand jury for neglecting a ferryboat, improperly grinding corn, or not penning in swine. And in a mark of the Puritan culture, grand jury inquiries in Plymouth kept watch over the morality of the colony, issuing indictments for drunkenness, obscene speech, breaking the Sabbath, excessive frivolity, and idle living.

All 13 American colonies had some form of the grand jury by 1683. As the colonies flourished, so did the grand jury's role as a government watchdog over everyday matters. The Connecticut grand jury ensured children were taught to read and helped local officials levy taxes. In Maryland, the grand jury often surveyed land and helped settle boundary disputes. New Jersey's grand jury was empowered by the colony's assembly in 1694 to not only levy taxes but also keep track of their use in each county. New Jersey grand jurors also inspected roads and bridges and often complained about their conditions.

Soon colonists recognized the power of grand juries to defy royal authority, especially as resentment grew over Britain's taxes and trade regulations that inevitably favored the king over the resource-rich colonies. By refusing to issue a true bill, for example, a grand jury could block enforcement of British laws, in much the same way as the Protestant-leaning grand jury in England had defied Charles II nearly a century earlier. The first recorded act of mutiny by an American grand jury against British officials was in the colony of Georgia in 1741: Jurors demanded a full accounting of the funds sent to their colony and, unsatisfied with the British response, began swearing in their own witnesses.

When the local court dismissed them from duty, they continued to meet in private homes. Among other demands, the Georgia colonists wanted more land, the right to own slaves, and a representative assembly.

Boston grand jurors followed suit in 1765 by refusing to indict leaders of the Stamp Act riots, in which colonists protested the first direct taxes levied by Parliament upon the colonies. The Stamp Act was designed to maintain the colonial military establishment by taxing newspapers, magazines, legal documents, insurance policies, dice, and playing cards. Boston grand jurors also refused to indict local newspaper editors for libel in 1768. The following year, they took a proactive stance both by denouncing British soldiers for harassing residents and by accusing the local prosecutor of "having received so many lucrative court favors."

In the escalating dispute with England, grand juries' actions became popular mediums of propaganda, and many pro-independence leaders used grand jury hearings as forums for making impassioned speeches. By 1770, a Philadelphia grand jury that had started out investigating local abuse of England's tea tax was promoting union with other colonies to seek redress of collective grievances. In 1775—just a year before the United States declared its independence—a Delaware grand jury voted for a tax to defend that colony and others against England. In Rhode Island, meanwhile, grand jurors were expected to turn in anyone still loyal to the king.

Leaders of the American Revolution considered the grand jury such an essential part of individual freedom against official tyranny that they encoded it in the Bill of Rights as they drafted and revised the U.S. Constitution. The Fifth Amendment reads, "No person shall be held to answer for a capital, or otherwise infamous crime, unless on a presentment or indictment of a Grand Jury, except in cases arising in the land or naval forces, or in the Militia, when in actual service in time

American colonists burn English tax stamps to protest the Stamp Act of 1765. Boston grand jurors went against the wishes of their English governor by refusing to indict the leaders of Stamp Act protests.

of War or public danger."

Some historians argue that after the American Revolution, the grand jury never developed into the consistently neutral buffer between government and individuals the Founding Fathers had envisioned. Instead, such detractors say, grand juries have too often mirrored popular prejudices in their decisions. Throughout the 1700s, for example, grand jury indictments reflected the battle between Federalists and Republicans, the nation's earliest political parties. More recently, President Clinton and his supporters maintained that the Starr investigation and resulting impeachment hearings in Congress were motivated by pure partisan politics. It is interesting to note that when the House formally impeached the President in its historic 1999 action, the vote was almost perfectly split along party lines.

After the Civil War, when the Ku Klux Klan formed to intimidate newly freed black slaves, Southern grand juries so stubbornly refused to indict KKK members and enforce the rights of African Americans to vote that Congress empowered federal courts to step in and conduct grand jury investigations of their own. Few local grand juries in the Reconstruction South were willing to interfere with their towns' chapter of the KKK, whose hooded henchmen have become synonymous with cross-burnings and lynching. Sometimes, grand juries withheld indictments for fear of reprisal. More commonly, however, the decisions of local grand juries throughout the South reflected widespread anger about losing the Civil War, economic devastation, and increased competition for jobs with freed blacks. One local grand jury in Blount County, Alabama, went so far as to indict a large number of people who opposed the Klan. Another local grand jury inspired a South Carolina courtroom to erupt in cheers when it refused to indict Klan members. Meanwhile, federal grand juries, whose panelists were carefully screened to include newly freed blacks, liberally indicted Klan members and others who threatened, attacked, and even murdered nonwhite citizens. One federal panel in Raleigh, North Carolina, indicted 750 people following a KKK raid on the town of Rutherford. Although most of those charged never actually stood trial, federal authorities hoped the grand jury's action would serve as a strong deterrent.

In the 19th century, serving on a grand jury was considered a privilege. Jurors living in rural areas of the country often traveled long distances to serve. This illustration from Harper's Weekly shows the jurors' sleeping quarters in one West Virginia trial.

As the KKK prosecutions demonstrate, grand juries have also reflected the unique geographic and cultural challenges of each region as the United States grew and expanded westward. On the American frontier, grand jury indictments for gambling and public drunkenness, dueling and carrying concealed weapons, selling liquor without a license, and horse and cattle rustling underscored the West's lack of traditional values and rough-hewn way of life. "Hardly a grand jury met on the frontier that did not return indictments for profane swearing," notes one historian.

Today's jurors may complain about the inconveniences of serving, interruptions to busy schedules, and long commutes to the courthouse. But grand jurors in newly settled territory often carried out their duties under harsh and dangerous conditions, traveling by horse or foot on poor roads to an unheated log cabin that served as the courthouse. Because of the lack of accommodations, an entire court in the Dakota Territory—including jurors, witnesses, lawyers, and judges—spent nights together on a cabin courthouse's mud floor. A Kansas grand jury slept in a pile of hay. Sometimes, grand juries withdrew to nearby woods to deliberate in secret as local ranchers and their families gathered around the courthouse out of curiosity and boredom. Court days on the isolating frontier were often an excuse to network pioneer-style—to leave work for a day, have a picnic, catch up on gossip, maybe trade some livestock. Grand jurors themselves passed the downtime during their tenures by whittling, chewing tobacco, and frequenting taverns. Sometimes they were dismissed from duty by the judge because they were unable to sober up. Grand jurors drank together to initiate new panelists and they drank together to celebrate the end of court sessions. The lawyers involved with one Houston County, Texas, grand jury in 1838 treated the panelists to drinks until they became "gloriously drunk." Yet for all their foibles and crudeness, grand juries helped maintain law and order and often served as the only government bodies on the open frontier.

Once the territorial stage of western regions passed and those areas became states, many dropped the traditional local grand jury system, citing all the same reasons critics use today: that the system is inefficient, expensive, too vulnerable to local whim, and too easily used against political enemies. In the last half of this century, federal grand juries in particular have been criticized as instruments of oppression, most notably during the anti-Communist hysteria of the 1950s led by Senator Joseph McCarthy. But some of the greatest abuses came two decades later, during the presidential tenure of Richard Milhous Nixon.

STRONG ARM
OF THE LAW

Richard Nixon waves farewell as he leaves the White House in disgrace on August 9, 1974. During Nixon's term as president, the grand jury system was used to attack his political enemies.

Perhaps no other chapter in American history more keenly demonstrates the grand jury's potential for abuse than that of the Richard Nixon administration (1969–74) and the political scandal known as Watergate, which forced President Nixon to resign. Many political scientists believe that the events of those five years, and their shocking disclosure in the news day after day, irrevocably poisoned Americans' trust of government and darkened experts' view of the grand jury system. One legal scholar, Leroy D. Clark, has argued that "the Nixon administration perverted the grand jury from its historic role of protection to one of harassment." Clark and many others feel that the inherently one-sided nature of grand juries—in which only the prosecution's case is presented—makes them perfect tools of oppression. Many critics of Starr's investigation of the Clintons found striking parallels with the Nixon administration's use of grand juries to intimidate and discredit political enemies.

Attorney General John Mitchell directed federal grand juries to interview ordinary citizens as a tactic to harass groups of people who disagreed with the government's policies.

Nixon was elected president in 1968, and reelected in 1972, during a time when America was deeply divided over the war in Vietnam, the civil rights movement, and changing values that included recreational drug use and extramarital sex. The assassinations of President John F. Kennedy, his brother Robert, and the Rev. Martin Luther King Jr. had been extremely traumatic to the American public. Many people found all the political and social upheaval very threatening, and Nixon was elected on a platform of restored "law-and-order." Of course, most crime is addressed on a local level and rarely affected by policies set in Washington. But Nixon's campaign promises appealed to a majority of voters and he appointed his friend and former law partner, John Mitchell, to be the nation's top prosecutor.

Soon it became clear that Attorney General Mitchell was as interested in prosecuting political criminals as he was in pursuing violent ones. Although the attorney general before him, Ramsey Clark, had found no legal basis to prosecute a group of student war protestors known as the Chicago Eight (arrested after disrupting the 1968 Democratic National Convention in Chicago), Mitchell quickly announced plans to prosecute them anyway. He also persuaded Congress to enact legislation—the Omnibus Crime Control and Safe Streets Act of 1968—that would authorize state and federal officials to wiretap, or secretly tape-record, the conversations of suspected criminals. The recorded information could then be presented to grand juries as evidence of wrongdoing. The measure was supposedly aimed at organized crime, but professional criminals quickly realized they were potential targets and figured out how to avoid undercover agents and "bugged" telephones. More often, wiretapped targets included left-wing writers and scholars, opponents of the Vietnam War, civil rights activists, and artists or intellectuals who had had little experience with the police and even less reason to suspect they might be under criminal investigation.

Critics of wiretapping argued that it violated innocent Americans' constitutional rights to privacy and free speech (imagine discovering that your parents or teachers had secretly recorded your most intimate conversations with friends about your hopes and fears, likes and dislikes). But Mitchell and others argued that wiretapping was necessary to maintain national security.

In 1969, tens of thousands of young people marched on the Pentagon to protest America's continued involvement in the Vietnam War. Mitchell claimed that national security was at stake, and ordered mass arrests of demonstrators and even bystanders in an effort to curb such public displays. Another key Nixon aide, Richard Kleindienst, had similarly promised a crackdown on "anarchistic kids" and "militants." A national program of suppressing dissent was being put into place.

Meanwhile federal grand juries across the country began summoning scores of people to testify about their beliefs, daily routines, conversations, and group memberships—as well as those of their friends and professional contacts. Sometimes the witnesses were called in connection with probes that had a legitimate origin, as in cases in which political extremists were planning bombings or other violent acts. But other times the probes became fishing expeditions with no purpose other than to harass and paralyze dissident groups. In 1969, for example, two members of the International Committee to Defend Eldrige Cleaver, a Black Panther member whom many people believed had been wrongfully accused of murder, were subpoenaed after their names appeared in a fund-raising ad in the *New York Times*. The government was seeking the names of other group members and volunteers, even though Americans are supposed to be able to join any group they choose, however repugnant its beliefs. When the two witnesses appealed to a higher court, the demand for their testimony was dropped.

In many other instances, though, subpoenaed witnesses who did not want to cooperate were threatened with contempt of court and perjury charges that could lead to imprisonment. One well-known investigative journalist of the period, Paul Cowan, reported in the *New York Times Magazine* in 1973 that 30 witnesses had been cited for contempt and 21 imprisoned by federal prosecutors. What made this tactic especially controversial was the fact that grand jury witnesses, because they had not yet been charged with a crime, did not have the same legal protections as targets. They could be subjected to unlimited searches of their property and to fingerprinting and voice printing—all of which could yield evidence that might be used against them. Witnesses also were not allowed to have a lawyer in the grand jury room with them as they testified, increasing the risk of incriminating themselves.

Even the lawyers of political radicals were summoned before Nixon-era grand juries, such as Black Panther defenders Sanford M. Katz and Gerald B. Lefcourt. This tactic—which was unusual at the time but has become much more common today—placed the lawyers in the unenviable position of having to choose between betraying their clients' confidentiality or being held in contempt of court. And for the first time ever, journalists and scholars critical of government policies were subpoenaed before grand juries to pressure them to reveal their confidential sources. One Harvard University professor, Samuel Popkin, became the first American scholar to be jailed for refusing to disclose his own official sources and name other academics and their sources. Popkin spent only a week in prison, thanks to the clout of Harvard, whose president, Derek Bok, met privately with Justice Department officials on Popkin's behalf. Using grand jury witnesses in this way not only disrupted the lives of individuals and deprived them of their civil rights, but hindered the effectiveness of groups whose members began distrusting each other.

In a few highly publicized cases, parents and children were pitted against each other to force one or the other to testify. Defense attorney Arthur Kinoy, who had represented several radical groups, including the Chicago Eight, was called before a grand jury to testify about his own daughter's antiwar activities at the University of Wisconsin. Kinoy tried to invoke attorney-client privilege but the court ruled that his testimony stemmed from his parental relationship, not his professional one. The court also found that parents and children were not protected from testifying against each other in the same way as husbands and wives. Kinoy was spared contempt charges when his daughter Joann turned up and appeared before the grand jury herself. Neither father nor daughter was ever convicted of a crime, and Kinoy says today he believes the entire episode was aimed at derailing his legal work on behalf of the Chicago Eight and other high-profile clients.

Similarly, the 15-year-old son of Daniel Ellsberg was subpoenaed to testify against his father, who was being prosecuted for his role in releasing the so-called Pentagon Papers to the press. The Pentagon Papers were a massive Defense Department study, classified as top secret, that detailed the nation's growing involvement in Southeast Asia. The study documented how several administrations had misled the public about the reasons for the Vietnam War and its consequences— including the number of American casualties. Ellsberg, a Harvard scholar, high-level government analyst, and former Marine, had actually been invited to help with the study. But he ultimately leaked the Pentagon Papers to the *New York Times* because of his growing conviction that the Vietnam War effort was futile.

As a result, Ellsberg became the target of an FBI investigation and federal grand jury probe in Los Angeles that led to his indictment on treason charges. At one point, his son was subpoenaed at 7 o'clock in the morning to appear before the grand jury by 10 A.M. that same day, leaving him virtually no time to consult a lawyer. Ultimately, as in the case of the Kinoys, the case against Ellsberg was dismissed after it was disclosed in court that two high-level Nixon aides had broken into the office of Ellsberg's psychiatrist in search of discrediting information. (The same two men, Howard Hunt and G. Gordon Liddy, would later be convicted in the Watergate scandal.)

The broad questioning of witnesses during the Nixon era transformed the federal grand jury from a

panel meant to investigate past events to one used for collecting information for future use. Some historians believe that this did not happen randomly but was part of a centrally directed plan by the Nixon administration to use grand juries as an intelligence-gathering network. As evidence, legal scholars cite the revival of the Justice Department's Internal Security Division (ISD), a handpicked team of federal prosecutors that was formed during the anti-Communist hysteria of the late 1940s and 1950s. ISD's use had waned but in late 1970, the ISD's staff suddenly increased 1,000 percent, from 6 to 60 lawyers. The ISD controlled grand jury investigations in 36 states and 84 cities during Nixon's tenure, even though the standard practice had always been for locally assigned federal prosecutors to handle matters in their jurisdictions. And although the usual

Dr. Daniel Ellsberg speaks with reporters outside the U.S. Courthouse in Los Angeles about the Pentagon Papers case.

conviction rate was 65.2 percent at the time, only 10 percent of the ISD's 200 indictments resulted in conviction, Clark found. Those indictments resulted from at least 100 grand jury investigations involving 1,000 to 2,000 witnesses over a three-year period. Later, when Nixon himself was under investigation for the Watergate matter, congressional testimony revealed that the man in charge of security for Nixon's 1972 reelection campaign—James McCord—had had regular access to ISD files that were supposed to be highly restricted. That proved that information gathered during the supposedly confidential grand jury process was instead being used for political purposes.

McCord himself became one of the officials convicted in the Watergate scandal; another was the ISD's director, Robert Mardian. The scandal began in June 1972, just months before the November presidential election, when a group of men were caught red-handed breaking into the Democratic National Committee's office in the Watergate building, a luxury apartment house and hotel on the Potomac River in Washington, D.C. It soon became evident that the burglary was no routine crime. No cash or items of value had been taken from the office but its files had been disturbed. As the public would learn thanks to the relentless reporting of two *Washington Post* writers, Bob Woodward and Carl Bernstein, the break-in was organized not by ordinary street thugs but by members of the Committee to Re-elect the President (CRP), an organization with close ties to the Nixon administration. The Watergate break-in also turned out to be just one of many illegal acts carried out to place Democrats and other political enemies at a disadvantage and ensure reelection of the "law-and-order" president.

A federal grand jury was convened to review the Watergate burglary but, in the hands of Nixon administration prosecutors, was accused of conducting a cover-up. For one thing, even though the Watergate burglars were arrested on June 17, 1972, they were not indicted until Sept. 15, 1972—possibly to make sure the matter would not go to trial before the November election. With most Americans still unaware of CRP's role in the burglary on election day, Nixon was easily reelected with 68 percent of the vote. Also, one of the federal prosecutors on the case was routinely updating the White House on the grand jury's progress, even though grand jury proceedings are supposed to be confidential. As the grand jury investigation progressed, the defendants also received special treatment. Reelection committee official Maurice Stans was allowed to file a sworn statement with the court rather than appear before the grand jury to testify, and John W. Dean III, one of Nixon's top aides, wasn't called as a witness even though he was said to have conducted his own investigation of the break-in for the White House.

Finally, rather than pursue the premise that the burglary was part of Nixon's underground reelection campaign, the prosecutors tried their case on the theory that break-in mastermind G. Gordon Liddy was trying to blackmail Democratic Party officials for private financial gain. It was only after Congress began conducting its own hearings on the matter, and a special prosecutor was appointed to revive the criminal investigation, that a number of Nixon's top aides were indicted in the scandal and Nixon resigned the presidency, on August 9, 1974, rather than face impeachment hearings.

Nixon was by no means the first leader to take advantage of the grand jury's broad powers and use them to disarm political opponents. Abraham Lincoln ordered the arbitrary arrests of so many people opposed to the Civil War that Congress responded with the Habeas Corpus Act of 1863, directing that all political prisoners be released unless they were indicted by a grand jury. President Franklin D. Roosevelt ordered grand jury indictments of fascist propagandists opposed

As the Watergate scandal mushroomed, President Nixon attempted to reassure the American people that he had not been involved in "dirty tricks." But the growing volume of evidence forced him to resign the presidency in order to avoid impeachment and possible removal from office.

to America's involvement in World War II. And during the cold war, conservatives led by Senator Joseph McCarthy used grand juries to root out Communist sympathizers in ways that foreshadowed the Nixon administration's tactics. (As a young congressman, Nixon himself had been an ally of McCarthy as a member of the House Un-American Activities Committee.) But President Nixon's grand jury abuses, coming as they did in modern times, on the heels of the civil rights movement, and in the age of television, evoked public anger as never before. Although an effort to reform the federal grand jury system failed, a number of states modified the local grand jury process in the wake of the Nixon years.

POWER TO THE PEOPLE?

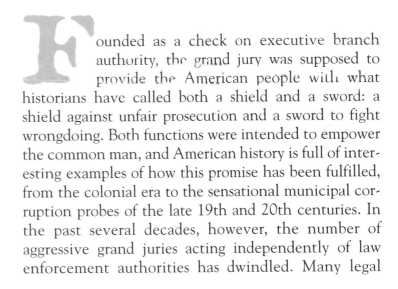

ounded as a check on executive branch authority, the grand jury was supposed to provide the American people with what historians have called both a shield and a sword: a shield against unfair prosecution and a sword to fight wrongdoing. Both functions were intended to empower the common man, and American history is full of interesting examples of how this promise has been fulfilled, from the colonial era to the sensational municipal corruption probes of the late 19th and 20th centuries. In the past several decades, however, the number of aggressive grand juries acting independently of law enforcement authorities has dwindled. Many legal

The 1735 trial of John Peter Zenger, a printer and publisher in colonial America, was important in establishing the American tradition of freedom of the press. Zenger's trial was held after two colonial grand juries refused to indict him on charges of publishing seditious libel, despite pressure from British officials.

experts fear that, for a variety of reasons, the Founding Fathers' planned voice of the community has largely been muted and that the institution is no longer working as intended.

The grand jury seems to have acquired its watchdog and quasi-lawmaking roles during colonial times, when the absence of established police forces and legislatures enabled these panels to not only return indictments sought by the king's agents but also to bring presentments stemming from their own knowledge. As chapter 4 explained, grand juries reviewed local finances and insisted on better roads and bridges, among other basic services, at a time when lawmakers were based in faraway England. In a significant stance that deserves a closer look, grand juries also resisted British authority by refusing to indict accused dissidents such as John Peter Zenger.

Zenger was the publisher of the *New York Weekly Journal*, a newspaper that was critical of colonial New York's governor, William Cosby, who had been appointed by King George II of England. In 1734, a judge and ally of the governor asked a grand jury to indict those who had been circulating seditious libel— material that could inspire rebellion. It was obvious the judge's unnamed target was Zenger, but the grand jury refused to indict him. The judge then asked a second grand jury to indict Zenger, this time naming the newspaperman directly and submitting as evidence two satirical songs published in the *Journal*. The grand jury issued an indictment but did not name a defendant, claiming it was impossible to pin down the identity of the songs' author, printer, or publisher. A frustrated Cosby then bypassed the grand jury system entirely, charging Zenger with the crimes himself. Cosby's action only eroded his public support at a time of growing distrust of the British. Zenger, meanwhile, was found not guilty by a trial jury in 1735. His case became legend and no doubt helped convince the Founding

CAUTION!!

COLORED PEOPLE

OF BOSTON, ONE & ALL,

You are hereby respectfully CAUTIONED and advised, to avoid conversing with the

Watchmen and Police Officers of Boston,

For since the recent ORDER OF THE MAYOR & ALDERMEN, they are empowered to act as

KIDNAPPERS

AND

Slave Catchers,

And they have already been actually employed in KIDNAPPING, CATCHING, AND KEEPING SLAVES. Therefore, if you value your LIBERTY, and the *Welfare of the Fugitives* among you, *Shun* them in every possible manner, as so many *HOUNDS* on the track of the most unfortunate of your race.

Keep a Sharp Look Out for KIDNAPPERS, and have TOP EYE open.

APRIL 24, 1851.

A poster distributed by minister and abolitionist Theodore Parker. Even though Parker's efforts to end slavery and to protect runaway slaves violated existing federal laws, a grand jury reviewing his case in Boston, where many people opposed slavery, refused to indict the minister.

Fathers to include the right to grand jury indictment in the Bill of Rights.

Clearly, the grand jury worked as a bulwark against British authority and helped the United States achieve independence. Later, when the issue of slavery dominated the national agenda, the case of Boston minister Theodore Parker affirmed the value of review by a grand jury as a protection against unjust prosecution. Parker was a popular crusader against laws that allowed the arrest of runaway slaves and their return to Southern masters. Courthouse riots often erupted during this time as passionately committed abolitionists tried to protect fugitive slaves and police had little choice but to arrest them. In the wake of one such brawl, Parker was accused of obstructing justice by preventing a U.S. marshal from carrying out his duties. The case was presented to a grand jury, which refused to indict the clergyman. A second grand jury did indict Parker but he was never brought to trial. Whether legally right or wrong—Parker did, after all, break existing laws—the people had spoken through the grand jury and public opinion prevailed.

Grand juries also served as vehicles of protest on the American frontier, when once again the seat of power was far away and pioneers faced everyday nuisances and mortal danger with little government support. Grand juries in western territories deplored the lack of nearby post offices, called for army protection against marauding Indians, and decried official corruption in much the same manner as colonial grand juries had criticized their British rulers. The building of a road from the Miami River to Detroit, for example, was the subject of a grand jury probe into misappropriation of funds. In Mississippi Territory, grand jurors indicted a judge named Harry Toulmin on charges of helping Spain against the United States in the struggle to claim western Florida.

In the 1870s a Tucson, Arizona, grand jury exposed corruption among army officers who not only gave Indians arms and ammunition in exchange for fresh game—thus endangering the white settlers the soldiers were supposed to protect—but shamelessly exploited the Indians, too. The officers were plying Indian men with liquor and using Indian women as prostitutes, the grand jury revealed. And in Oregon, the spectacular disclosures of a grand jury's timberland probe—in which federal officers were accused of taking bribes in return for transferring public forests into private hands—inspired a series of pro-consumer investigations across the country.

Price fixing in the lumber, milk, fuel, farm machinery, meat, and sugar industries were among the misdeeds attacked by outraged grand jurors. In 1905, for example, a Chicago grand jury comprised of farmers and small businessmen indicted the officers of a meatpacking plant for cutting a sweetheart deal with the railroad. Chicago grand jurors had earlier unraveled a coal dealer's plot to drive up prices by destroying competition and creating an artificial shortage. One historian has noted that the coal retailer "had thousands of tons of coal at a time when families could not get enough fuel to heat their homes." Conflicts between industry and the growing labor movement also gave sympathetic grand juries plenty of opportunity to defend strikers and union organizers, as well as to root out graft among unscrupulous labor leaders.

As industrialization gave rise to America's great cities, fraud and corruption came to be regarded as a new version of tyranny and triggered grand jury probes across the country. San Francisco's grand jury gained status in the mid-19th century, as a voice of ordinary people fed up with graft. In a particularly western twist, in 1851 a vigilante branch of a San Francisco grand jury formed to bring justice to the killer of a dry goods store owner when corrupt police failed to do the job. Five years later, the vigilantes reunited after the murder of a crusading newspaper editor. San Francisco was also the scene of a protracted grand jury probe into the control of city hall by various utilities—including the city's famed trolley system, whose executives were paying off public officials to ensure they obtained the rulings they needed. Intrepid San Francisco grand jurors continued investigating even after the devastating earthquake and fire of 1906 forced them to meet in makeshift offices.

But probably the best-known municipal corruption case undertaken by a grand jury was the one that

Thomas Nast's cartoons in Harper's Weekly drew attention to William Marcy "Boss" Tweed's illegal activities, but it took a grand jury investigation to put the corrupt political leader in jail.

brought down New York City's infamous Tweed Ring. This political "machine" was run by William Marcy Tweed, an alderman, state senator, and U.S. congressman. The Tweed Ring controlled jobs, elections, and judges in New York while raiding city coffers. Tweed's most ambitious scheme to rob the city treasury came in 1868, with the construction of a new courthouse in New York County. The work was expected to cost $500,000; by 1871, more than $8 million in public tax money had been spent and the building was not yet completed.

The cartoons of Thomas Nast, appearing in *Harper's Weekly*, stirred public indignation about the misappropriation of funds, and an exposé was published in the *New York Times*. However, all had failed to unseat the Tweed Ring when the grand jury began its probe in November 1871.

The Tweed grand jury gathered evidence without the support of the prosecutor's office, which was controlled by the ring and tried to stymie the investigation. Determined and well organized, the jurors split up into committees of two or three people. Using the grand jury's power of subpoena, and supported by Tweed's political enemies, the jurors visited banks to check on the accounts of public officials, interviewed witnesses at their homes if they were too frightened to testify at the courthouse, and studied the operations of each city department.

The grand jurors faced bribes and threats as they carried out their task. When a legal technicality threatened to end the grand jury's term, allies in the state legislature in Albany intervened so the jurors could keep investigating. Tweed and a dozen cronies were finally indicted on charges of grand larceny and conspiracy. After the grand jury completed its investigation in February 1872, a judge told the jurors they had just finished "one of the most important, extraordinary and eventful sessions that has ever marked the history of an American grand jury." Tweed eventually was convicted and sentenced to 12 years in prison; he spent most of the rest of his life in jail.

A subsequent New York City grand jury probe looked at the failure of another corrupt city hall administration to crack down on a slew of illegal gambling halls that were draining workingmen's pockets and generating a host of other crimes. Once again, a corrupt prosecutor tried to sabotage the effort; the police department went so far as to prepare a dummy list of gambling halls to throw the grand jury off track. But this grand jury had a strong leader in its foreman, publisher George H. Putnam, who was financially independent and enough of a community pillar in his own right to stand up to authorities. When witnesses began disappearing or hesitated to talk in front of the prosecutor, for example, the grand jury began to subpoena witnesses directly and even demanded that the prosecutor leave the room during some testimony. When a corrupt local judge ignored a grand jury report concerning sabotage by the police and prosecutor, Putnam forwarded a copy directly to New York's governor, Theodore Roosevelt. Roosevelt finally removed District Attorney A. B. Gardiner from office in 1900 after New York City's police chief was indicted. A grand jury had once again prevailed.

The citizens of Minneapolis also benefited from a strong grand jury foreman, a local businessman named Hovey C. Clark. When the county prosecutor's office refused to help the grand jury investigate the administration of Mayor Alfred A. Ames during an era of rampant local crime, Clark hired his own private detectives to hunt down evidence. Scouring the city, Clark's private eyes found two petty thieves willing to testify that they helped collect the fees Ames and his police chief brother extracted from criminals in exchange for shielding them from arrest. The grand jury was able to follow a money trail leading from the collectors, or so-called big mitt men, all the way to Ames's office and that of his brother, Police Chief Fred Ames. Both brothers were indicted and the mayor was forced to resign.

The Ames brothers' demise took place in 1902. Decades later, the administration of President Richard Nixon was similarly brought down after the arrest of four burglars at Washington's swanky Watergate apartment house led to indictment of key political figures and finally, the resignation of the president himself.

In this case, however, it was the Pulitzer Prize–winning reporting of the *Washington Post*, not a grand jury probe, that traced an exchange of money up the political ladder and exposed how Nixon and his aides had illegally sabotaged their rivals. Subsequent hearings before Congress also helped ferret out details and bring them to the public's attention.

But in terms of the grand jury's function, the Watergate case was a turning point away from public power. For one thing, the scandal underscored how easily the President and his aides had used their power, including law-enforcement tools like grand juries, for personal, political gain. And in the hands of government prosecutors, the federal grand jury charged with investigating the break-in proved fairly useless until an independent special prosecutor was brought in to direct the probe.

The Watergate grand jury ultimately indicted Nixon's closest aides—including the nation's top law-enforcement officer, Attorney General John Mitchell. In doing so, it helped send the message that no one is above the law. The Watergate grand jury also deserves credit for helping to prepare an important report detailing the scandal that was released to the House Judiciary Committee and thus made a matter of public record. But the Watergate episode also demonstrated just how prosecutor-dependent the institution had become.

Assertive, history-making grand juries have become increasingly rare during the 20th century. Susan Brenner, an associate dean at the University of Dayton Law School, believes grand juries have gradually faded into anonymity as cities have grown and residents have become more isolated from each other. In small towns 100 years ago, Brenner believes, citizens knew each other well, knew what was going on in each other's lives and at the local courthouse, and were more likely to speak up against wrongdoing. Today, we have become more cynical and self-protective. Although we hear about trial juries all the time because they are featured on TV, the secrecy of grand jury proceedings has protected them from similar publicity. The grand jury has simply faded from public view, and thus from the public's conscience. When grand jurors are impaneled, they follow the model of trial jurors because that's what they know from TV. They listen quietly and passively, raising no questions till the deliberation phase, even though, in Brenner's words, grand juries should be "rambunctious and obstreperous." Brenner noted that, a few years ago, the State of Hawaii gave grand juries their own attorneys to represent their interests, independent of local law-enforcement authorities. The Hawaii legislature believed grand juries had become too passive in the hands of prosecutors.

The change from proactive to passive grand juries might be traced to the 1930s, when the Justice Department grew exponentially in response to new federal regulations and criminal laws, according to another law professor, Jonathan Turley of George Washington University Law School. Today, Turley notes, the U.S. Department of Justice is a mammoth institution with branches in every state. Literally thousands of government lawyers make their living pursuing cases ranging from tax resisting to drug trafficking, discrimination to pollution. At the same time, changes to the federal rules governing criminal procedures have curtailed grand jurors' discretion to summon and question witnesses on their own. Over time, Turley and others believe, the power over grand jury proceedings shifted from the jurors themselves to the prosecutors—in other words, from the layperson to the professional. That is the opposite of the system envisioned by the Founding Fathers. But it is a trend that was compounded during the government's War on Drugs, when Congress and the Supreme Court scaled back suspects' rights in favor of victims' rights and police discretion to fight crime. A major consequence is that the grand jury is now widely regarded as little more

than a rubber stamp, a nuisance to participants that is an unnecessary step in the justice system.

One notable exception has been the recent "runaway grand jury" in Denver, Colorado, whose defiance of federal prosecutors brought the grand jurors themselves under criminal investigation. Known as the Rocky Flats grand jury, the panel's name comes from a nuclear weapons plant outside Denver, a facility owned by a major arms manufacturer—Rockwell International—with millions of dollars in government contracts. The jurors were impaneled in 1989 to review alleged violations of environmental laws, including nuclear waste contamination, at the Rocky Flats plant. But when the U.S. Attorney's Office decided to settle the case out of court—fining Rockwell $18.5 million but bringing no criminal charges against any of its officers—the jurors accused prosecutors and other

It was the work of Washington Post reporters Carl Bernstein (left) and Bob Woodward that brought the Watergate scandal to the public's attention; a grand jury impaneled to investigate wrongdoing in the Nixon administration was ineffective.

Jim Stone, a former engineer with Rockwell International, arrives in court to testify in the environmental case against the company. The so-called runaway grand jury's investigation into violations of environmental laws at Rockwell's Rocky Flats facility is sealed by judicial order; the members of the grand jury have sued so that their findings can be made public.

government officials of a cover-up.

In 1992, holding a news conference on the steps of the federal courthouse, they declared their independence from prosecutors and thus became what is known as a "runaway," or out-of-control, grand jury. After they disbanded and started giving interviews—breaking grand jury secrecy rules—the jurors themselves came under the scrutiny of the FBI. They hired Turley as their defense lawyer and managed to quash the FBI investigation. Then, in 1996, the grand jurors took the unprecedented step of filing a federal lawsuit seeking permission to reveal the findings of their Rocky Flats investigation. At this writing, the case is still pending and has been placed under seal by a federal judge, meaning no one involved is allowed to discuss its details. If the jurors win, it would mark the first time that such a panel's findings are disclosed without benefit of an indictment. Many Americans are eagerly awaiting the outcome of this extraordinary episode in modern legal history, a case that could return the grand jury to its populist roots.

TRADITION AND REFORM

Grand juries have been a part of the American justice system since colonial days. Today, many observers feel that the system must be reformed.

From the moment grand juries were encoded in the Bill of Rights, lawyers, politicians, and scholars have argued about their value. Americans, it seems, have never been completely comfortable with the secrecy of the proceedings or their one-sided nature. The cost of maintaining grand juries and the pressure to continuously find fresh panelists have also been cited as burdens outweighing any perceived benefits. Indeed, most states no longer use local grand juries to bring routine criminal charges, and others, such as New York, have altered their rules to even the playing field between prosecutors and the defense. Americans have not been alone in their misgivings: England, where the grand jury originated, abandoned the system decades ago. In the United States, the grand jury has endured, but continues to thrust lawmakers into cycles of debate between tradition and reform, as the furor surrounding the Kenneth Starr investigation illustrates so colorfully.

87

Felix Frankfurter (1882–1965) was appointed to the U.S. Supreme Court in 1939 and served until 1962. Prior to his appointment to the nation's highest court, Frankfurter opposed the grand jury system and recommended that it be abolished.

Immediately after the American Revolution, local grand juries were held in high esteem, thanks to their role in defeating British rule. But as soon as the framers of the Constitution created the federal grand jury system—by incorporating the right to grand jury indictment into the Bill of Rights in 1791—mistrust of centralized power was roused once more. Many citizens viewed the federal courts—and by extension, their grand juries—as too reminiscent of the royal courts once imposed on American colonies.

In newly formed states, meanwhile, opinion varied as to how much power even local grand juries should enjoy. A major sticking point was the ability of grand jurors under the common law of that time to indict someone on their own knowledge, without any additional evidence or witnesses. The guaranteed right to indictment became a hot topic at several ratifying conventions and not every state constitution included the phrase. One prophetic Pennsylvania judge warned of the potential dangers of unlimited grand jury investigations and suggested they first receive court approval. (Court approval for every grand jury used by a prosecutor was actually required in Pennsylvania until the mid-1970s, when state laws were changed to make grand jury use more common. Today, both grand juries and preliminary hearings are used in that state.) Another colonial-era lawyer from Pennsylvania, Edward Ingersoll, expressed the concerns of the time by arguing that the secrecy of the grand jury and power of its members to indict based on their own knowledge was "at variance with all modern English theory of judicial proceedings." In 1821 the Louisiana legislature decided to bar the state's grand juries from initiating any investigations of their own and confined them to acting only on indictments presented by a prosecutor. In 1859, Michigan became the first state to stop using state and local grand juries altogether.

Across the Atlantic, English legal reformers had

been calling the grand jury a corrupt system that favored the upper classes. The notion of random selection was still unheard of and those chosen to serve tended to be friends of the court. Critics also argued that even the wealthy property owners generally appointed to grand jury duty did not have the legal training to adequately scrutinize evidence. Justice would be better served, the argument went, if trained law-enforcement authorities were the ones to review criminal charges. In 1859—the same year Michigan abolished the state and local grand jury—Parliament passed England's Vexatious Indictments Law, which curbed the power of grand juries by requiring private citizens to present their suspicions to a police magistrate, not a grand jury. The magistrate would then determine whether or not the accusations deserved to go before a grand jury.

England's anti–grand jury movement inevitably influenced scholars and writers in this country, where at least one magazine urged American judges to follow their British counterparts and take an active stand against grand juries in their courtrooms. But the outbreak of the Civil War in 1861 pushed the grand jury debate to the bottom of the nation's agenda. Arbitrary arrests and other abuses of military rule during wartime also reaffirmed the value of grand juries to screen cases and protect individuals from government whim.

The next big push to abolish grand juries came in the 1920s and 1930s, when the effects of the Great Depression gave new urgency to claims that the system was expensive and inefficient. Future Supreme Court justice Felix Frankfurter was among those calling for an end to grand juries, arguing that the trial courts could provide protection enough against malicious prosecution. His arguments were supported by a 1931 project sponsored by the Social Science Research Council, a survey that became a centerpiece of the national debate. The study, which was carried out by a Columbia

The indictment of gangster Charles "Lucky" Luciano in 1936 was one of several high-profile cases during the 1930s that helped ensure that grand juries would continue to be impaneled.

University professor and a dean from the University of Oregon, compared three states that used grand juries to bring routine criminal charges with three states that did not. Echoing earlier criticism, the survey concluded that using panels of ordinary citizens was a less efficient way to screen criminal evidence than having professionals conduct a review. Grand juries took too long to look at cases and were hampered by their lack of legal training, the survey found. It also dismissed most grand juries as being little more than convenient tools for prosecutors—either enabling them to obtain indictments whenever they wanted or to provide convenient scapegoats for charges that proved unjust.

But the grand jury system survived, in America at least. A series of successful, highly publicized corruption cases in the 1920s and 1930s captured the nation's imagination and helped raise public opinion about the value of grand juries. In perhaps the best-known case, a New York grand jury indicted famed gangster Charles "Lucky" Luciano, breaking up a racketeering ring that had been extorting millions of dollars a year from city officials and taxpayers. Similar grand jury probes in Kansas City, Chicago, and Pittsburgh also exposed rampant criminal activity and official corruption. Together, these cases reinforced the idea that even ordinary citizens had the power to keep government and big business in check.

Exploiting these successes, a New York–based network of former grand jurors organized to counter any attacks on the system. At the time, grand jury alumni were proud of their involvement and had often served multiple terms. They were viewed as part of an elite group and were a political force of their own. They mounted a vigorous public relations campaign that emphasized the attractive, quintessentially American notion of an empowered citizenry. At the same time, many areas of the western United States that had neglected to use the grand jury system were falling victim to encroaching railroads, utilities, and other monopolies and finding themselves with little recourse. Those abuses by big business, coupled with the rise of dictatorships in Europe, seem to have served as daily reminders that the rights of ordinary individuals were more important than efficiency, and that the grand jury could still serve as a bulwark against such despotism.

In England, World War I and an economic depression had the opposite effect. Parliament had suspended the use of grand juries in 1917 in the face of war with

Germany and the imminent shortage of men to serve as jurors. The use of grand juries never resumed. Citing the Depression, Parliament officially abolished grand juries in 1933.

The American grand jury system wasn't seriously scrutinized again until the 1970s, in the wake of the Watergate scandal that forced President Nixon to resign and exposed his use of law-enforcement tools (wiretapping, grand jury investigations) to harass government critics. This time, the debate shifted from economics to civil rights as the public reacted to documented violations of privacy and free speech. As one critic wrote, the grand jury's "protective function has been trivialized and the investigator's function expanded to the point where the institution is almost precisely the opposite of what the Founding Fathers intended."

In 1974—the year of Nixon's resignation—the American Bar Association formed a special grand jury committee to study potential reforms. Its focus was on changing the rules and procedures of the federal grand jury to better protect the individual—not only targets of inquiries but witnesses, too. A priority was an examination of the rule excluding defense lawyers from the grand jury room, which forced witnesses to either interrupt their testimony to consult with their attorneys outside or risk exposing themselves to criminal charges. Another key issue was the ability of prosecutors to introduce evidence to the grand jury that would not be allowed at trial, such as information gained through the use of wiretaps. Reformers also felt that witnesses should be reminded of their right not to incriminate themselves, in a Miranda-like warning similar to the one issued upon arrest. And reformers wanted witnesses to have access to transcripts of their testimony, to help protect them from perjury charges later on.

The Bar Association's Grand Jury Committee issued 30 "legislative principles," or recommended rules, that incorporated all those protections, and more. Most were adamantly opposed by the Department of Justice and although Congress held hearings on the matter, no changes were enacted. Remarkably, federal grand juries have continued to operate much as they did in the 18th century. Several states responded to the Bar Association's effort with reforms of their own. New York, for example, gives defendants the right to testify before the grand jury and allows their defense lawyers to be present in the grand jury room. In fact, any witness before a New York grand jury may bring counsel into the grand jury room. But the movement to reform grand juries waned during the 1980s, when the epidemic use of cocaine and crack cocaine led to

This 1970 photo of attorney Gerald Lefcourt was taken during a trial in which he defended several members of an African-American militant group, the Black Panthers. Lefcourt is in favor of reforming the grand jury system; he and other attorneys have proposed significant changes to the federal grand jury system.

rising crime rates. Once again, concerns about personal safety superseded those of individual liberty. Politicians seemed more reluctant than ever to enact any changes that would diminish the power of prosecutors.

Today, partly inspired by the Starr inquiry, a new movement is under way to reform the federal grand jury system. A leader of the effort is Gerald Lefcourt, the Manhattan-based lawyer who defended Black Panthers and other radicals during the 1960s and 1970s and who was among the first wave of lawyers to be subpoenaed to testify against clients. (Calling lawyers before grand juries, especially when their clients are accused drug dealers, became a common practice during the government's War on Drugs of the 1980s.) These days,

Lefcourt's clients are more likely to include wealthy businessmen fighting tax evasion or racketeering charges than political dissidents. But he and other defense lawyers believe prosecutors have gained an unfair share of power over the grand jury process. As a past president of the National Association of Criminal Defense Lawyers, he has launched a campaign to win many of the same reforms that fizzled more than 20 years ago.

Lefcourt believes Congress today may be more sympathetic to changing the grand jury system than it was after Watergate. A big reason is that many politicians themselves have been prosecuted on charges ranging from racketeering to sexual harassment—often at great personal cost and at the expense of their careers. And prosecutors have been criticized for using high-profile cases to launch political careers of their own; New York mayor Rudolph Giuliani, for example, was a federal prosecutor who made headlines by investigating people ranging from former Miss America Bess Meyerson to Mafia leader John Gotti. In addition, the ability of prosecutors to seize convicted drug dealers' homes and cars even after they are sentenced to prison—a power gained during the War on Drugs—has rankled even conservatives who view the extra punishment as a form of double jeopardy.

Lefcourt and his group have drafted a proposed "Bill of Rights" for the federal grand jury system. The proposed changes include the following:

- Allowing all witnesses the right to bring a lawyer into the grand jury room while they testify
- Giving all witnesses, before they testify, a Miranda-type warning (informing them of their right to an attorney, to remain silent, and to not incriminate themselves)
- Giving all witnesses at least 72 hours' notice before they have to appear before a grand jury

- Giving all witnesses the right to obtain a transcript of their grand jury testimony (at their own expense)
- Giving better instructions to the grand jurors about their duties and powers and the charges they are to consider
- Giving the targets of grand jury investigations the right to testify and offer their own information by approaching the foreperson, in writing
- Barring federal prosecutors from intentionally using illegally seized information, or other evidence that would not be allowed at trial, to secure an indictment
- Barring federal prosecutors from intentionally withholding information that could clear the subject of a grand jury investigation
- Barring federal prosecutors from naming "unindicted coconspirators," which unfairly taints a person without bringing criminal charges against him or her
- Barring federal prosecutors from calling as a witness anyone they know will invoke their Fifth Amendment right not to testify, because doing so prejudices the grand jury

In New York, meanwhile, a committee named by the state's top judge recently recommended a series of changes aimed at making grand jury service less burdensome. The study, touted as the first of its kind, took about 18 months to complete and was based on 5,000 surveys as well as a public hearing. With more than 25,000 grand jurors sworn in each year, New York's system is the largest in the nation. The goal is to enable all types of people to serve—and thus produce more diverse grand juries—by reducing the length of service. The committee also proposes increasing stipends from $40 a day to $60 a day and even $80 a day for those serving more than 20 days, fees that would be the high-

The motto over the entrance to the U.S. Supreme Court building in Washington, D.C. Ultimately, the goal of the grand jury system is to ensure that the rights of all citizens are respected.

est of their kind if approved by the state legislature. Other recommendations include cleaning up many of the state's decrepit grand jury chambers and bathrooms, and allowing grand jurors to phone in before they report to the courthouse, so they can make sure the prosecutor is ready to present his or her cases. The study found that 25 to 50 percent of grand jurors' time was spent waiting around, rather than hearing evidence. That kind of waste not only hampers the court system and costs taxpayers, but leaves a bad impression with the public, officials noted as they released their report.

"We want to put our best foot forward," New York chief judge Judith S. Kaye said at a news conference. "For many citizens, this is their only exposure to the justice system." Later, Kaye said that calls to abolish the New York grand jury system, which peaked during the late 1980s and early 1990s, never gained enough support to actually generate the necessary legislation. Neither prosecutors nor defense lawyers were eager to abandon an institution that had existed since New York was a colony. Yet, Kaye noted, "no attention was being given to improving the current system."

Judge Kaye's extremely practical approach and Lefcourt's legalistic one illustrate the tug-of-war that has been at play since the American grand jury's inception. One camp emphasizes expense and efficiency. The other places priority on civil liberties. Both recognize the vital role of citizens in the process and the need to treat them with respect, whether they are grand jurors who want access to clean bathrooms, or witnesses demanding ready access to their lawyers. Both approaches also assume that it is unlikely the grand jury will be abolished any time soon—only modified in response to historical events.

♠   ♠   ♠

Monica Lewinsky's graphic testimony about her affair with President Clinton, and the nasty maneuvering that compelled her to testify before the grand jury, marked a milestone in the history of this unique institution. For many people, the treatment of Lewinsky and her relatives, as well as the treatment of other, innocent witnesses in the case, exemplified the type of government abuse the Founding Fathers had hoped to prevent. Prying into the president's sexual escapades in such detail also offended many Americans' rock-solid belief in the right to privacy, even if they were not Clinton supporters and did not approve of his adulterous behavior. As a result, Congress allowed the statutes authorizing the unfettered investigative powers of the Office of the Independent Counsel to expire—meaning that Kenneth Starr could well become the last special prosecutor of his kind. And yet even the outrages of the Lewinsky affair prompted few, if any, calls to dismantle the grand jury system itself. Thus the Starr investigation illustrated not only the workings and foibles of the grand jury, but its ambivalent place in American society.

Bibliography

American Bar Association. *Grand Jury Policy and Model Act (1977–1982)*. Washington, D.C.: Section of Criminal Justice, 1982.

———. *Frequently Asked Questions About the Grand Jury System*. Washington, D.C.: Division for Media Relations and Public Affairs, 1998.

Blank, Blanche Davis. *The Not So Grand Jury: The Story of the Federal Grand Jury System*. New York: University Press of America, 1993.

Brenner, Susan W., and Gregory C. Lockhart. *Federal Grand Jury: A Guide to Law and Practice*. Cleveland: West Group, 1996.

Bruni, Frank. "Indictment Was Possible, Clinton Grand Juror Says." *The New York Times*, 26 March 1999.

Clark, LeRoy D. *The Grand Jury, The Use and Abuse of Political Power*. New York: New York Times Book Co., 1975.

Emerson, Deborah Day. *Grand Jury Reform: A Review of Key Issues*. Washington, D.C.: The U.S. Department of Justice, National Institute of Justice, Office of Development, Testing, and Dissemination, 1983.

Kinoy, Arthur. *Rights on Trial: Odyssey of a People's Lawyer*. Lexington, Mass.: Bernel Books, 1983.

Lefcourt, Gerald B. "High Time for a Bill of Rights for the Grand Jury." *The Champion* (April 1998).

Leipold, Andrew D. "Why Grand Juries Do Not (And Cannot) Protect the Accused." *Cornell Law Review* 61, no. 1 (January 1995).

Morse, Wayne L. "A Survey of the Grand Jury System." *Oregon Law Review* 10, no. 2 (February 1931).

Morton, Andrew. *Monica's Story*. New York: St. Martin's Press, 1999.

Rudenstine, David. *The Day the Presses Stopped: A History of the Pentagon Papers Case*. Berkeley, Calif.: The University of California Press, 1996.

Schlesinger, Arthur M. jr., general editor. *The Almanac of American History*. New York: Barnes and Noble Books, 1993.

Younger, Richard D. *The People's Panel: The Grand Jury in the United States*. Providence, R.I.: American History Research Center, Brown University Press, 1963.

Index

Index

LESLIE BERGER is an award-winning journalist who covered courts and cops, including the Rodney King beating and the 1992 Los Angeles riots, for the *Los Angeles Times*. She currently is a freelance writer in New York City, where she lives with her husband and two sons.

AUSTIN SARAT is William Nelson Cromwell Professor of Jurisprudence and Political Science at Amherst College, where he also chairs the Department of Law, Jurisprudence and Social Thought. Professor Sarat is the author or editor of 23 books and numerous scholarly articles. Among his books are *Law's Violence, Sitting in Judgment: Sentencing the White Collar Criminal,* and *Justice and Injustice in Law and Legal Theory.* He has received many academic awards and held several prestigious fellowships. He is President of the Law & Society Association and Chair of the Working Group on Law, Culture and the Humanities. In addition, he is a nationally recognized teacher and educator whose teaching has been featured in the *New York Times*, on the *Today* show, and on National Public Radio's *Fresh Air*.

Picture Credits